Excel 2002

Level 3

Allison K. P. Clark

Excel 2002: Level 3

Part Number: 084202
Course Edition: 3.2

ACKNOWLEDGMENTS

Project Team

Curriculum Developer and Technical Writer: Allison K. P. Clark • **Content Manager:** Cheryl Russo • **Copy Editor:** Christy D. Johnson • **Technical Editor:** Rachel L. Chaffee • **Print Designer:** Dan Smith

NOTICES

HELP US IMPROVE OUR COURSEWARE

Your comments are important to us. Please contact us at Element K Press LLC, 1-800-478-7788, 500 Canal View Boulevard, Rochester, NY 14623, Attention: Product Planning, or through our Web site at **http://support.elementkcourseware.com**.

This logo means that this courseware has been approved by the Microsoft® Office Specialist Program to be among the finest available for learning Microsoft Excel 2002. It also means that upon completion of this courseware, you may be prepared to take an exam for Microsoft Office Specialist qualification.

What is a Microsoft Office Specialist? A Microsoft Office Specialist is an individual who has passed exams for certifying his or her skills in one or more of the Microsoft Office desktop applications such as Microsoft Word, Microsoft Excel, Microsoft PowerPoint, Microsoft Outlook, Microsoft Access, or Microsoft Project. The Microsoft Office Specialist Program typically offers certification exams at the "Core" and "Expert" skill levels. The Microsoft Office Specialist Program is the only program in the world approved by Microsoft for testing proficiency in Microsoft Office desktop applications and Microsoft Project. This testing program can be a valuable asset in any job search or career advancement.

To learn more about becoming a Microsoft Office Specialist, visit **www.microsoft.com/officespecialist**. To learn more about other Microsoft Office Specialist approved courseware from Element K, visit **www.elementkcourseware.com**.

*The availability of Microsoft Office Specialist certification exams varies by application, application version, and language. Visit **www.microsoft.com/officespecialist** for exam availability.

Microsoft, the Microsoft Office Logo, PowerPoint, and Outlook are trademarks or registered trademarks of Microsoft Corporation in the United States and/or other countries, and the Microsoft Office Specialist Logo is used under license from owner.

Element K is independent from Microsoft Corporation, and not affiliated with Microsoft in any manner. This publication may be used in assisting students to prepare for a Microsoft Office Specialist Exam. Neither Microsoft, its designated program administrator or courseware reviewer, nor Element K warrants that use of this publication will ensure passing the relevant exam.

NOTES

EXCEL 2002: LEVEL 3

CONTENTS

APPENDIX A: MICROSOFT OFFICE SPECIALIST PROGRAM

Notes

ABOUT THIS COURSE

Now that you have completed the first two levels of Excel 2002, you are ready to continue on to the third level. You already know the basic and some advanced operations in Excel, now you will learn even more.

You have learned the basics of using Excel and can employ most of its features. In this course, you will learn about some of Excel's more advanced functionality, thereby rounding out your skill set.

Course Description

Target Student

Persons desiring to prepare to be a certified Microsoft Office User Specialist (MOUS) in Excel at the expert level and who already have knowledge of the Microsoft Windows 98 or above operating system, and an intermediate knowledge of Excel 2002.

Course Prerequisites

To ensure your success, we recommend you first take the following Element K courses or have equivalent knowledge:

- *Windows 2000: Introduction*
- *Excel 2002: Level 1*
- *Excel 2002: Level 2*

How to Use This Book

As a Learning Guide

Each lesson covers one broad topic or set of related topics. Lessons are arranged in order of increasing proficiency with *Microsoft Excel*; skills you acquire in one lesson are used and developed in subsequent lessons. For this reason you should work through the lessons in sequence.

We organized each lesson into results-oriented topics. Topics include all the relevant and supporting information you need to master *Microsoft Excel*, activities allow you to apply this information to practical hands-on examples.

You get to try out each new skill on a specially prepared sample file. This saves you typing time and allows you to concentrate on the skill at hand. Through the use of sample files, hands-on activities, illustrations that give you feedback at crucial steps, and supporting background information, this book provides you with the foundation and structure to learn *Microsoft Excel* quickly and easily.

As a Review Tool

Any method of instruction is only as effective as the time and effort you are willing to invest in it. In addition, some of the information that you learn in class may not be important to you immediately, but it may become important later on. For this reason, we encourage you to spend some time reviewing the topics and activities after the course. For additional challenge when reviewing activities, try the What You Do column before looking at the How You Do It column.

As a Reference

The organization and layout of the book makes it easy to use as a learning tool and as an after-class reference. You can use this book as a first source for definitions of terms, background information on given topics, and summaries of procedures.

Course Objectives

In this course, you will customize your workbook, work with multiple data sources, and collaborate with others using shared workbooks. You will also enhance your worksheets using charts and graphic objects.

You will:

- customize your workbook by applying conditional formatting, adding data validation criteria, customizing menus and toolbars, creating and editing a macro, and grouping and outlining structured data.

- work with multiple workbooks to create a workspace, consolidate data, link cells, edit links, export Excel data into XML, import XML data into Excel, and create a Web query.

- collaborate with other Excel users by protecting your workbook, sharing your workbook, setting revision tracking, merging multiple copies of the same workbook, and tracking changes.

- chart non-adjacent data, modify chart items, and create a trendline.

- use multiple graphic objects to enhance your worksheet.

Course Requirements

Hardware

- A Pentium 133 MHz or higher processor required for all operating systems.
- A minimum of 64 MB of RAM, recommended, for Windows 2000 Professional; in addition, you should have 8 MB of RAM for each application running simultaneously.
- A minimum of 516 MB of free hard disk space. (Under Windows 2000, at least 4 MB of space must be available in the Registry.)
- Either a local CD-ROM drive or access to a networked CD-ROM drive.
- A floppy-disk drive.
- A two-button mouse, an IntelliMouse, or compatible pointing device.
- A VGA or higher-resolution monitor; Super VGA recommended.
- An installed printer driver.
- A sound card.

Software

- A custom installation of Microsoft Office XP Professional—see the Class Setup Requirements for additional instructions.

Class Setup

This book was written using the Windows 2000 Professional operating system. Using this book with other operating systems may affect how the activities work. Note: The manufacturer states that Microsoft Office XP Professional with FrontPage will work with Microsoft Windows 98, Microsoft Windows ME, and Microsoft Windows NT Workstation 4.0. Office XP Professional with FrontPage will not run on the Microsoft Windows 3.x, Microsoft Windows NT 3.5x, or Microsoft Windows 95 operating systems.

1. Install Windows 2000 Professional on a newly formatted hard drive.
2. If the Getting Started With Windows 2000 window is displayed, uncheck Show This Screen At Startup and click Exit.
3. Install a printer driver.

    A printer isn't necessary for class, but you must have a printer driver installed.

4. A complete installation of Microsoft Office XP Professional with FrontPage.

    Steps 1 through 4 need to be done only once. Steps 5 through 7 must be done before every class to ensure a proper setup.

5. On the students' computers, reset the usage data. (Choose Tools→Customize and click Reset My Usage Data to restore the default settings.)
6. Delete the folder C:\My Documents\Excel. Delete the folder C:\XML Data.

7. Run the self-extracting data file located on the data disk. This will place the data in the My Documents folder. (Verify where you want the data files located.) Move the XML Data folder to the C drive.

LESSON 1

Customizing your Workbook

Lesson Objectives:

In this lesson, you will customize your workbook by applying conditional formatting, adding data validation criteria, customizing menus and toolbars, creating and editing a macro, and grouping and outlining structured data.

You will:

- Apply conditional formatting to a range of cells.
- Add data validation criteria to a range of cells.
- Customize existing menus and create your own menu.
- Customize the toolbars.
- Create a macro.
- Edit a macro.
- Add group and outline criteria to a range.

Introduction

Now that you have a good understanding of how to work in and with workbooks and worksheets, it is time to learn how to customize these workbooks and worksheets to meet your specific viewing and editing needs. In this lesson you will customize your workbook by applying conditional formatting, adding data validation criteria, customizing menus and toolbars, adding and running macros, and viewing your data using outlines.

Imagine that you are in charge of updating an Excel workbook on a regular basis. This workbook used to be managed by someone else, so the workbook isn't set up the way you usually set up your own workbooks. The person who owned the workbook before you made some changes to the workbook; you may want to modify it to meet your business needs.

TOPIC A

Apply Conditional Formatting

One way to customize your worksheet is to apply conditional formatting to cells so that if they meet the specified criteria, they appear as you would like them to. In this topic, you will apply conditional formatting to a range of cells.

Imagine that you are working in a worksheet that contains hundreds of entries of sales data. Every month you have to give a presentation on the sales results of each division. You want to point out any department that is above its quota for the month and you do that by bolding and changing the font color on all the sales numbers that are above the quota number. So, every month you have to find the departments that are above quota, highlight the text, bold it, change the text color to red, and then move on to the next one. Some months you are changing 20 or more numbers! You can do this in Excel with conditional formatting.

What is Conditional Formatting?

Definition:

Conditional formatting is a format that Excel automatically applies to specified cells if the criteria that are placed on that cell are met.

Example:

If you have a worksheet that contains the sales information for various sales reps and you want to call out when they have not met their quota for sales, you could apply conditional formatting to the sales column so that any number that fell below the quota number would be made bold and blue.

Analogy:

Conditional formatting is like being at a family reunion where everyone who has married into the family has to wear a purple scarf so they can easily be identified as non-blood family.

Apply Conditional Formatting

Procedure Reference: Conditional Formatting

To apply conditional formatting:

1. Select the cell or cells that you want to apply the formatting to.
2. Display the Conditional Formatting dialog box.
3. Set the criteria for the formatting.
4. Display the Format Cells dialog box.
5. Select the formatting you want and click OK.
6. Click OK.

ACTIVITY 1-1

Applying Conditional Formatting

Data Files:

- Office Supplies.xls

Setup:

Excel is running and no files are open.

Scenario:

You have the file (Office Supplies) that summarizes total amounts spent on office supplies in the four divisions of your company. Because of budget constraints, anyone who is spending over $1500 a quarter needs to be notified. You want to call out these numbers by applying conditional formatting to the totals for each division so that any quarter total that is above $1500 appears in red and is italicized to draw attention to those numbers. When you are finished you will save the file as My Office Supplies.

LESSON 1

What You Do	How You Do It

1. On the Australian Sheet tab, **select the quarter totals** and in the Conditional Formatting dialog box, **set the first condition so that the formatting will be applied if the cell value is greater than 1500.**

    a. **Open the file Office Supplies.**

    b. **Select the Australian Sheet** if necessary.

    c. **Select the range B9:E9.**

    d. **Choose Format→Conditional Formatting.**

    e. In the first drop-down list, **verify that Cell Value Is is selected.**

    f. From the second drop-down list, **select Greater Than.**

    g. **Place the insertion point in the last box and type** *1500*.

2. **Set the formatting so that the cells will be italicized and the cell text will be red.**

    a. **Click the Format button.**

    b. On the Font tab, in the Font Style list, **select Italic.**

    c. From the Color drop-down list, **select a shade of red.**

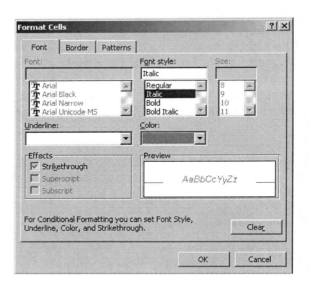

    d. **Click OK.**

3. **Apply the conditional format to the text by changing some of the numbers in the data and change one of the numbers above 1500 to a number below 1499.** When you are finished, **save the file as *My Office Supplies*.**

a. **Click OK to apply the conditional formatting.** Notice that when you apply the conditional format, the numbers that are above 1500 are red and italicized.

b. **Change the number in cell B4 to *800*. Press [Enter].** The Qtr1 total is now red and italicized.

c. **Save the file as *My Office Supplies*.**

TOPIC B

Add Data Validation Criteria

Another way that you can customize your worksheet is by adding data validation criteria to cells that you frequently enter the wrong type of data in. In this topic, you will add data validation criteria to a range of cells.

Imagine that you are working in a worksheet that you frequently use. This worksheet contains text and numbers, but you find that you are constantly entering text into cells that should only contain numbers. You never realize your mistake until you have entered a lot of data and you have to go back, find the mistake, and fix it and everything that is linked to it. What if you could make those cells only accept numbers so that it would be impossible for you to enter the wrong type of data? In Excel, you can do just that by adding data validation criteria to a cell or range of cells.

What is Data Validation?

Definition:

Data validation is a set of criteria you place on a cell or range of cells that prevents anything other than what meets the criteria from being entered in that cell or range of cells. Each data validation rule has three parts. The first part is the criteria that define a valid entry. The second part is a message (which is optional) that appears when a user selects the cell that contains the rule. The third part is an error message that appears when a user enters invalid data.

Example:

If you have a worksheet that contains information on personnel within your company and you want to ensure that only the state abbreviation, two characters, can be entered into the State column, you can set a data validation rule that will only allow two characters in the cells in this column.

Add Data Validation Criteria

Procedure Reference: Create a Data Validation Rule

To create a data validation rule:

1. Select the range that you want to apply the data validation to.

2. Display the Data Validation dialog box.

3. Set your criteria for a valid entry.

4. If desired, create an optional message on the Input Message tab.

5. If desired, make changes to the default error message on the Error Alert tab.

6. Click OK.

ACTIVITY 1-2

Creating a Data Validation Rule

Setup:

The file My Office Supplies.xls is open.

Scenario:

When you are using this file, sometimes you mistype and end up placing text in the cells where you only want numbers. So, you will create a data validation rule that will only allow numbers in the data area. When you are done, you will save the file.

What You Do	How You Do It
1. Select the data for the four quarters on the Australian sheet and display the Data Validation dialog box.	a. On the Australian sheet, **select the range B4:E7.**
	b. **Choose Data→Validation** to display the Data Validation dialog box.

To put error msg.

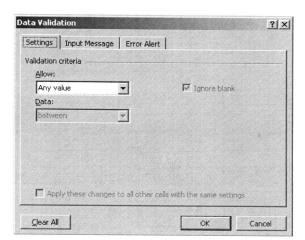

2. **Set the validation criteria to a decimal between 0 and 10000. Use Figure 1-1 and Figure 1-2 to set the input message and error alert.**

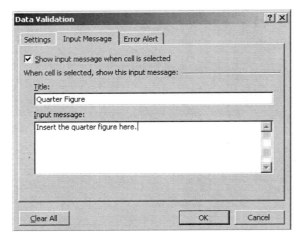

Figure 1-1: *The input message.*

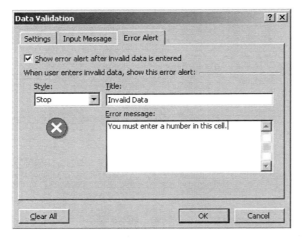

Figure 1-2: *The error alert.*

a. On the settings tab, from the Allow drop-down list, **select Decimal.** From the Data drop-down list, if necessary **select between.** In the Minimum text box, **type 0** and in the Maximum text box, **type 10000.** This will allow any number between 0 and 10000 to be entered into the cells.

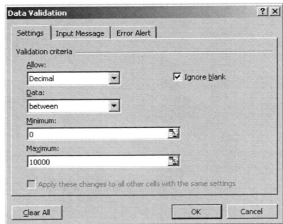

b. On the Input Message tab, in the Title text box, **type *Quarter Figure.*** In the Input Message text box, **type *Insert the quarter figure here.***

c. On the Error Alert tab, from the Style drop-down list, if necessary **select Stop.** In the Title text box, **type *Invalid Data.*** In the Error Message text box, **type *You must enter a number in this cell.***

d. **Click OK.**

3. **What happens when you select a cell and try to enter some text, rather than a number into one of the data cells?**

TOPIC C

Customize Menus

In addition to customizing your data, you can also customize your workbook environment. One of the most useful features of Excel is the ability to customize your menus. In this topic, you will add a custom menu that contains menu choices you use frequently in your workbook.

When you are working in Excel, are there menu choices that you use frequently? Imagine how much more productive you would be if you had all of those frequently used menu choices on one, easily, accessible menu. In Excel 2002, you can do just that.

Customize Menus

Procedure Reference: Create and Customize Menus

To create and customize a menu:

1. Open the Customize dialog box.
2. Select the Commands tab.
3. From the Categories list, select New Menu.
4. From the Commands list, drag the New Menu to the menu bar.
5. Select the categories and commands that you want to place on the menu and drag the commands to the new menu.

ACTIVITY 1-3

Customizing Menus

Setup:

My Office Supplies.xls is open.

Scenario:

Since you find yourself working with Excel more and more, you want to create a menu that will house all of the menu choices that you use most frequently. These include saving the workbook, closing the workbook, printing the workbook, cut, copy, and paste. You will call the menu My Menu and when you have finished creating your custom menu, you will observe the changes and then you will delete it.

What You Do	How You Do It
1. Open the Customize dialog box, and create a new menu next to the Help menu on the Menu bar.	a. Choose Tools→Customize and select the Commands tab.

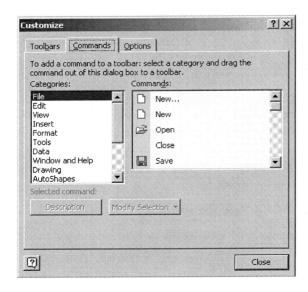

b. In the Categories list, **scroll down and select New Menu.**

c. From the Commands list, **drag the New Menu to the menu bar and place it next to the Help Menu.**

2. Add the following commands to the New Menu: Save, Close, Print, Cut, Copy, and Paste.

a. From the Categories list, **scroll up and select File.**

b. In the Commands list, **select the Save command and drag it over the New Menu on the menu bar. When the New Menu drops-down, place the Save Command in the drop-down menu area.**

c. Add the Close command in the same way, under the Save command.

d. In the Categories list, **select Edit.**

e. Add the Cut, Copy, and Paste commands to the new menu.

3. Change the name of the New Menu to *My Menu*. When you are finished, look at your new menu.

a. **Right-click on the New Menu.**

b. In the Name text box, **select the text New Menu and type** *My Menu*.

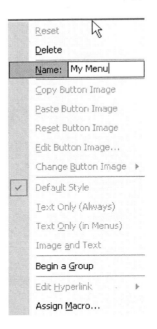

c. **Click Close in the Customize dialog box.**

d. **Display the My Menu menu.** You now have your own custom menu.

4. **Delete the custom menu.**

Normally, when you create a custom menu, you don't delete it right away. You are deleting it here for class purposes.

a. **Choose Tools→Customize.**

b. **Drag the My Menu menu off the menu bar onto a blank area in the workspace.**

c. **Click Close.**

TOPIC D

Customize Toolbars

Now that you know how to customize your workbook by adding custom menus, you will want to know how to customize toolbars. In this topic, you will learn how to customize the toolbars by adding and deleting toolbar buttons.

Nothing is worse than clutter when you are trying to get something done. Have you ever noticed how many toolbar buttons there are and how few you actually use? Well, in Excel you can remove the toolbar buttons you don't use, and add ones that you would use.

Customize Toolbars

Procedure Reference: Customize Toolbars

To customize existing toolbars by adding and deleting toolbar buttons:

1. Open the Customize dialog box.
2. Select the Commands tab.
3. Drag the desired buttons from the Commands list to the toolbar to add a button.
4. Drag the unwanted buttons to the workspace to delete them.
5. Click Close.

ACTIVITY 1-4

Customizing Toolbars

Setup:
My Office Supplies.xls is open.

Scenario:
You have found when you are working in Excel, that many of the buttons on the toolbar do not get used. You would like to remove some of these button so you can reduce some of the on-screen clutter. You will remove the E-mail, Search, and Insert Hyperlink buttons and then you will add the Protect Sheet button next to the Save button. When you have finished, you will reset all toolbars to their default state.

What You Do	How You Do It
1. Open the Customize dialog box and from the Standard toolbar, remove the E-mail, Search, and Insert Hyperlink buttons from the toolbar.	a. Choose Tools→Customize. b. From the Standard toolbar, **drag the E-mail** [button] **button off the toolbar into the workspace.** c. **Drag the Search** [button] **button off the toolbar.** d. **Drag the Insert Hyperlink** [button] **button off the toolbar.**
2. Add the Protect Sheet button to the toolbar, placing it next to the Save button. Observe the changes to the toolbar.	a. From the Categories list, **select Tools.** b. From the Commands list, **scroll down and select the Protect Sheet command. Drag the command to the toolbar, and place it next to the Save button.** c. **Click Close.**
3. Reset the toolbars.	a. **Choose Tools→Customize.** b. **Click on the Toolbars tab.** c. **Verify that Standard is selected in the Toolbars list and click Reset.** d. **Click OK.** e. **Click Close.**

TOPIC E

Create a Macro

Another way to customize your workbook to make working in it more efficient is to create and run macros for the tasks you frequently perform. In this topic, you will create and run a macro.

Imagine that you have a workbook that contains multiple worksheets. On each of these worksheets you want to bold the text in cell A1 and add a color to it. Then you want to format the data cells so that they appear as currency. Finally, you want to add bold and italics to the headings. You think you are going to have to perform each individual keystroke on each worksheet within your workbook. You can create a macro that will do all of this for you in one easy step.

What is a Macro?

Definition:

A macro is a group of user-created instructions that automates one or more operations. In Excel 2002, you use the computer programming language Visual Basic for Applications to create macros.

Example:

Imagine that every time that you create a new worksheet in Excel, the first thing you do is insert the company logo into cell A1, change the font of the entire worksheet to Times New Roman and change the font size to 8pt. In Excel, you create a macro that will do all of this for you automatically.

Analogy:

A macro is like a housekeeper. You explain all of the things you want the housekeeper to do to clean your house once, and then when you ask him to "clean the house," he will do it exactly the way you showed him following all the instructions you provided automatically.

Create Macros

Procedure Reference: Create a Macro

Anytime you find yourself performing repetitive keystrokes or tasks, consider recording your keystrokes as a macro. To create a macro by recording it:

1. Open the Record Macro dialog box.

2. In the Macro Name text box, type the name of your new macro.

3. Perform the keystrokes that you want to automate.

4. Click the Stop Recording button.

ACTIVITY 1-5

Creating and Running a Macro

Setup:

The file My Office Supplies.xls is open.

Scenario:

In your file My Office Supplies, you want to add color and increase the font size of the cell that contains the title, bold and italicize the column headings, and format that data to currency. Rather than have to perform the keystrokes on each sheet, you will create a macro named My_Macro that does all of these things for you. You will then run this macro on the European worksheet and finally save the file.

What You Do	How You Do It
1. Open the Record Macro dialog box and name the new macro *My_Macro*.	a. Choose Tools→Macro→Record New Macro.
	b. In the Macro Name text box, **type My_Macro.**
	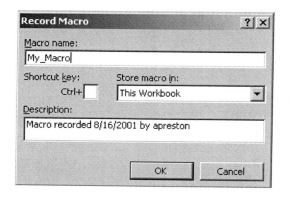
	c. **Click OK.**
2. While recording the macro, **format cell A1 to be 18 pt with a text color of blue.**	a. **Select cell A1.**
	b. From the Font Size drop-down list, **select 18.**
	c. From the Font Color drop-down list, **select blue.**

3.	Add bold and italics to the column headings.	a.	Select the range A3:E3.
		b.	Click the Bold button.
		c.	Click the Italic button.

4.	Apply currency formatting to the quarter data.	a.	Select the range B4:E7.
		b.	Select Format→Cells.
		c.	On the Number tab, in the category list, select Currency.
		d.	Click OK.

5.	Stop recording the macro, and run the macro on the European worksheet. Save the file when you are finished.	a.	Click the Stop Recording ■ button.
		b.	Click on the European sheet tab.
		c.	Choose Tools→Macro→Macros.
		d.	Verify that My_Macro is selected and click Run.
		e.	Save the file.

TOPIC F

Edit a Macro

Now that you have learned how to create and run a macro, you will want to know how to edit one in case you need to update an existing macro. In this topic, you will learn how to edit an existing macro using the Visual Basic Editor.

So you have created your macro. What happens though if you need to add an action to it, or change an existing action? Do you have to delete the macro and start from scratch? You can just edit the existing macro to suit your changing needs.

Edit a Macro

Procedure Reference: Edit a Macro

To view and edit a macro in Visual Basic Editor:

1. Choose Tools→Macro→Macros.

2. In the Macro list, select the Macro you want to edit.

3. Click Edit.

4. Make the changes to the macro in the Visual Basic Editor window.

5. Click the Save button.

6. Close Visual Basic Editor and return to Excel.

Viewing Macro Code

After recording a macro, not only can you run the macro, but you can also examine and edit the macro code itself. The code can be viewed and edited in the Visual Basic Editor.

VBA code is stored in modules. Excel stores the modules with the workbook, and they open when the workbook opens. You can view modules by using the Visual Basic Editor, and selecting the module you would like from the Projects window.

Sub Procedures

A module sheet in an Excel workbook may contain many Sub procedures. A Sub procedure is a named sequence of statements that are executed as a unit. All executable code must be contained in a procedure. Some Sub procedures call (or refer to) only other Sub procedures. Sub procedure names must begin with an alphabetic character, cannot contain embedded periods or spaces, and must be unique.

Code Components

VBA code consists of statements and comment text. *Statements* are instructions executed when the macro is run. *Comment text*, which begins with a single apostrophe, is just a comment and it is not executed. The following table lists what statements consist of.

Statement Element	Explanation
Keywords	Terms that have special meaning in VBA. By default, keywords appear as blue text. For example, *Sub* and *End Sub* are keywords that mark the beginning and the end of a Sub procedure.
Operators	Used in much the same way as they are on a worksheet, they can be arithmetic (+,-), concatenation (&), logical (And, Or), or comparison (=, >, <).
Variables	A storage location that you designate with a unique name. The variable is usually modified during the execution of the Sub procedure.

Statement Element	Explanation
Procedure calls	You can place the name of a Sub procedure inside other Sub procedures. Some Sub procedures call only other Sub procedures.

ACTIVITY 1-6

Editing Macros

Setup:
The file My Office Supplies.xls is open.

Scenario:
You have spent some time creating your macro. There is only one problem; the font size you chose for cell A1 is too big. So, you are going to edit your macro so that the font size is 14 pt. When you are finished, you will save and close the file.

What You Do	How You Do It
1. Open the Macro dialog box and open the My_Macro macro in Visual Basic Editor.	a. Choose Tools→Macro→Macros.
	b. Verify that My_Macro is selected and click Edit.

2. Using the screen shot as a guide, **edit the macro so that cell A1 is 14 pt and the column heading range that is bolded and italicized is B3:E3.**

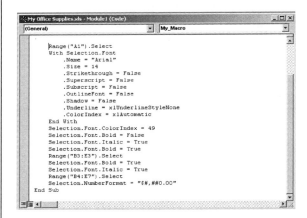

a. In the fourth line of the macro, **change the size to 14.**

b. In the line that contains the range A3:E3, **change the A to B so that the range reads B3:E3.**

---

3. **Save the changes to the macro and run the edited macro on the N. American worksheet.** When you are finished, **save and close the file.**

a. **Click the Save button.**

b. **Click the View Microsoft Excel button.**

c. **Select the N. American sheet tab.**

d. **Choose Tools→Macro→Macros.**

e. **Verify that the My_Macros macro is selected and click Run.** Notice that this time the font size in cell A1 is 14 and only the Quarter headings were bolded and italicized.

f. **Save and close the file.**

g. **Close Microsoft Visual Basic.**

TOPIC G

Group and Outline Structured Data

Another way you can customize your work space is by changing how you view your data. One way to view your data is to create an outline. In this lesson you will add group and outline criteria to a range.

Have you ever had a worksheet that contained so much data you had a hard time moving through it and finding the particular data that you wanted? Well, if that is the case then Outlining can help. Outlining your data makes it easier to move through and locate data in a large worksheet.

What is an Outline?

An outline is a structure that you add to your data that can have up to eight levels of information. You can show and hide each level of detail to make viewing large amounts of data easier.

Table 1-1: *The Outline Symbols*

Symbol	Description
Row- or column-level symbols	These symbols display numbers and appear above and to the left of the Select All box. You can display specific levels of outline information by clicking on these symbols.
Row- or column-level bars	These bars appear above the column headings and to the left of the row headings. They span the ranges grouped in an outline level (one end points to the first cell in the level, the other is immediately after the last cell in the level).
Hide detail symbols	These symbols appear as minus (-) signs and are used to hide rows or columns of information indicated by the row- and column-level bars.
Show details symbols	These symbols appear as plus (+) signs and are used to display hidden rows or columns of information.

Create an Outline

Procedure Reference: Create an Outline

To automatically create an outline structure for your worksheet data:

1. Select the range for which you want to create an outline. (To create an outline for the entire worksheet, you can select a single cell.)

2. Choose Data→Group And Outline→Auto Outline.

> ✎ If you don't want the outlining symbols to appear in your outline, choose Tools→Options and select the View tab. Under Window Options, uncheck Outline Symbols and click OK.

ACTIVITY 1-7

Creating an Outline

Data Files:

• Product Sales.xls

Setup:

Excel is running and no files are open.

Scenario:

You have a worksheet that contains a large amount of data. You frequently work in this worksheet and you would like to make it easier for navigating through and locating data. So, you will create an outline in the Product Sales file. When you are finished, your figure will look like Figure 1-3.

	A	B	C	D	E Qtr 1	F	G	H	I Qtr 2	J	K	L	M Qtr 3
1		Jan	Feb	Mar	Total	Apr	May	June	Total	July	Aug	Sept	Total
2	Sales												
3													
7	Total Books	$350	$525	$600	$1,475	$650	$600	$525	$1,775	$775	$775	$550	$2,100
8													
9													
10	Jazz	300	350	275	$925	300	325	300	$925	200	300	275	$775
11	Classical	325	325	250	$900	250	200	250	$700	250	325	250	$825
12	R&B	250	300	275	$825	200	250	225	$675	250	300	350	$900
13	Total CDs and Tapes	$875	$975	$800	$2,650	$750	$775	$775	$2,300	$700	$925	$875	$2,500
14													
15	Total Sales	$1,225	$1,500	$1,400	$4,125	$1,400	$1,375	$1,300	$4,075	$1,475	$1,700	$1,425	$4,600
16													
17													
18													
19													
20													

Figure 1-3: *Product Sales.xls after an outline has been created.*

What You Do	How You Do It

1. In the file, Product Sales.xls, what are some of the different ways you might like to view this information?

---

2. In the Product Sales.xls file, with cell A1 selected, **create an outline.**

   a. **Verify that cell A1 is selected.**

   b. **Choose Data→Group And Outline→Auto Outline.** The outline has been created.

---

3. **Using Table 1-1 as a guide, identify each of the outline symbols. Which symbols do you think you will use the most when you use the outlining feature?**

---

4. Using the outlining symbols, **expand and collapse all of the levels of the outline to view and hide the data. When you are finished, save the file as *My Product Sales*.**

a. **Click the column-level symbol 2.** The view included only quarterly and annual sales data.

b. **Click the column-symbol 1.** The view included only annual sales data.

c. **Click the column-level symbol 2,** to return to quarterly and annual sales data.

d. **Click the show detail symbol above column M.** This view includes data for only the third quarter.

J	K	L	M
			Qtr 3
July	Aug	Sept	Total
250	200	225	$675
300	325	175	$800
225	250	150	$625
$775	$775	$550	$2,100
200	300	275	$775
250	325	250	$825
250	300	350	$900
$700	$925	$875	$2,500
$1,475	$1,700	$1,425	$4,600

e. **Click the hide detail symbol above column M.** Excel collapses the third quarter.

f. **Click on the row-level symbol 2.** The view includes only summary data.

5. **Turn off your outline. Save and close the file.**

a. **Choose Data→Group And Outline→Clear Outline.**

b. **Save the file as *My Product Sales* and close the file.**

Lesson 1 Follow-up

In this lesson you have learned how to customize your workbook. You learned how to apply conditional formatting, add data validation criteria, customize menus and toolbars, create and edit macros, and group and outline structured data. You are now ready to customize your workbook making it more productive to work in Excel.

1. **Of the ways that you learned how to customize your workbook in this lesson, which do you think will be most useful to you and how will you use them?**

2. **What is one macro that you could create back at your office that would make your job easier? What are the tasks involved in that macro?**

LESSON 2
Working with Multiple Data Sources

Lesson Time
50 minutes to 60 minutes

Lesson Objectives:

In this lesson, you will work with multiple workbooks to create a workspace, consolidate data, link cells, edit links, export Excel data into XML, import XML data into Excel, and create a Web query.

You will:

- Create a workspace that includes multiple workbooks.
- Consolidate data by position and by category.
- Link cells in two different workbooks.
- Edit existing workbook links.
- Export an Excel worksheet as structured XML data.
- Import XML data.
- Create a Web query using XML data.

Introduction

By now, you should have a pretty good understanding of Excel and how to work with worksheets and workbooks. In this lesson, you will learn how to work with more than one workbook and data source by creating a workspace, consolidating data, linking cells, importing and exporting XML data, and creating a Web query using XML data.

Imagine having several workbooks and data that you work with frequently. Now imagine that you want to use information in each of the workbooks at the same time. This could be a very inefficient way of working with your data. In this lesson, however, you will learn how to efficiently use information from other workbooks and how to use multiple workbooks at once.

TOPIC A

Create a Workspace

One way to efficiently work with multiple workbooks is to create a workspace that contains many workbooks. In this lesson, you will begin working with multiple workbooks by creating a workspace.

Imagine that you come into work every day and open the same three workbooks that you work with throughout the day. Each day you need to resize each workbook window so they can all be seen in the same window. You spend about 10 minutes sizing and resizing so that it appears just perfect. Then, at the end of the day, you close all of the workbooks. The next day you come into work and have to do the same thing all over again. Wouldn't it be nice if you could save those display settings that you so meticulously set so that you don't have to do it over and over again? Well, you can by creating a workspace.

What is a Workspace?

A workspace is an Excel file that includes several workbooks. A workspace file allows you to open multiple workbooks in the same step. The workspace file contains location, screen size, and screen position data about each workbook. It doesn't, however, contain the actual workbook files. Workspaces make it easy to distribute uniform views of multiple files to multiple users on the same network.

Create a Workspace

Procedure Reference: Create Workspaces

To create a workspace file:

1. Open all the files that you want to include in the workbook.

2. Size and position the workbooks as you would like them to appear.

3. Choose File→Save Workspace.

4. In the File Name text box, name your workspace.

 When you save a workspace, you will notice that there is a different icon associated with the workspace than the usual Excel workbook icon.

5. Click OK.

 You open a workspace file the same way you open any other Excel file.

ACTIVITY 2-1

Creating a Workspace

Data Files:

*   Employee Personal.xls
*   Employee Benefits.xls
*   Employee Location.xls

Setup:

Excel is running and no files are open.

Scenario:

You are in charge of updating the employee information that is stored in three different workbooks. You have found that as your company grows you are using these three workbooks together all the time. So, you want to create a workspace called My Workspace from the files Employee Personal, Employee Benefits, and Employee Location and size them so that when you open the workspace all three workbooks are opened at the same time with the display intact.

What You Do	How You Do It
1. Open the files Employee Personal.xls, Employee Location.xls, and Employee Benefits.xls, and size the workbooks.	a. Choose File→Open. b. In the My Documents folder, **select Employee Benefits.** c. **Hold down the [Shift] key and select Employee Personal** to select all three files. d. **Click Open.**

2. **Arrange the windows vertically, so that they can all be seen at the same time.** Using the File menu, create a workspace, saving it as *My Workspace*.

   a. **Choose Window→Arrange.**

   b. **Select Vertical and click OK.**

   c. **Choose File→Save Workspace.**

   d. In the File Name text box, **type *My Workspace*.**

   e. **Click Save.**

🖈 With a workspace file, all the workbooks included are opened at the same time. However, when closing the workspace, all the workbooks need to be closed separately.

3. **Close the workbooks and then open the new workspace.** Notice that a workspace file is opened the same way that a workbook file is opened. When you are finished, **close all the open files without saving changes.**

   a. **Click the Close button on all the open workbooks.**

   b. **Choose File→Open.**

   c. **Select My Workspace and click Open.** Notice that all the workbooks were opened for you and they appear as they did when you saved them.

   d. **Close all the open workbooks.**

Topic B

Consolidate Data

Sometimes when you are working in one workbook, you will want to use data from other workbooks. In this lesson you will work with multiple workbooks by consolidating the data from several workbooks.

It is your job to summarize the sales report of three different sales reps. You have a sheet that you want to summarize the information on, so you assume that you need to open one workbook, copy the information from that workbook, close it, paste it into the summary workbook, and repeat those steps for all the workbooks you want to gather data from. Well, Excel lets you skip that long process. You can summarize the data from multiple worksheets into one worksheet quickly by consolidating the data.

What is Consolidating Data?

Consolidating data is the process of summarizing data from several ranges into a single range. The range data can come from the same worksheet, or workbook, or from different workbooks. You can consolidate data when the data has an identical structure (by position). You can also consolidate data when the data is similar, but in different relative locations, or the data has a different number of rows or columns in each category (by category).

Consolidate Data

Procedure Reference: Consolidate Your Data

You can consolidate your data by position or by category, and both are done similarly by selecting the area you want the consolidated data to appear in, and then selecting the data you want to consolidate. Once you have consolidated your data, viewing it is similar to the way you view an outline. To consolidate data:

1. Open all the files that you want to consolidate.

2. Select the worksheet and the cell or range of cells where you want the consolidated data to be placed.

3. Open the Consolidate dialog box.

4. Add all the ranges that you want to consolidate in the other worksheets.

5. Click OK.

ACTIVITY 2-2

Consolidating Data

Data Files:

*   Jaen.xls

*   Hanover.xls

*   Monder.xls

*   Consolidation.xls

Scenario:

You have three sales reports (Hanover, Monder, and Jaen) that need to be summarized. You have the report on which you want to consolidate the data (Consolidation.xls). You will consolidate the range C5:C14 on each of the worksheets in the Consolidation worksheet. When you are finished, save the file as My Consolidation and close the file.

LESSON 2

What You Do	How You Do It
1. Select the range where you want the consolidated data to be placed on the Consolidation worksheet.	a. Open the files Hanover, Monder, Jaen, and Consolidation.
	b. Activate the Consolidation workbook.
	c. Select the range C5:C14.

2. Using the Data→Consolidate menu command, **add the reference of C5:C14 on each of the three worksheets that contain data.**

a. **Choose Data→Consolidate.**

b. In the Consolidate window, next to the Reference text box, **click the Collapse Dialog** button. The Consolidate window is minimized, allowing you to select the range you want to be used as a reference.

c. **Switch to the Monder worksheet, select the range C5:C14, and press [Enter].**

d. **Click the Add button** to add the specified reference to the All References section.

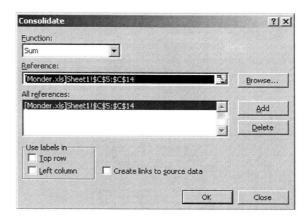

e. Use the same technique to **add the range C5:C14 on the Jaen and Hanover worksheets to the All References area.**

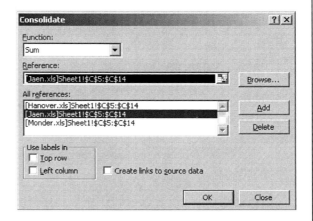

3. **Create links to the source data and finish the consolidation.** Observe the consolidated data. You will view the data in a later activity. When you are finished, **save the file as** *My Consolidation.*

a. **Check the Create Links To Source Data check box.**

b. **Click OK.** The consolidated data appears as an outline in the Consolidation worksheet.

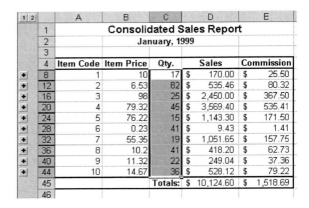

1 2		A	B	C	D	E
	1	Consolidated Sales Report				
	2	January, 1999				
	3					
	4	Item Code	Item Price	Qty.	Sales	Commission
+	8	1	10	17	$ 170.00	$ 25.50
+	12	2	6.53	82	$ 535.46	$ 80.32
+	16	3	98	25	$ 2,450.00	$ 367.50
+	20	4	79.32	45	$ 3,569.40	$ 535.41
+	24	5	76.22	15	$ 1,143.30	$ 171.50
+	28	6	0.23	41	$ 9.43	$ 1.41
+	32	7	55.35	19	$ 1,051.65	$ 157.75
+	36	8	10.2	41	$ 418.20	$ 62.73
+	40	9	11.32	22	$ 249.04	$ 37.36
+	44	10	14.67	36	$ 528.12	$ 79.22
	45			Totals:	$ 10,124.60	$ 1,518.69
	46					

c. **Save the files as** *My Consolidation.*

ACTIVITY 2-3

Viewing Consolidated Data

Data Files:

*   View Consolidated.xls

Setup:

The file My Consolidation.xls is open.

Scenario:

Now that you have consolidated your data, you want to view it so that you can verify your data. You will first display all the hidden data, then you will hide it.

What You Do	How You Do It
1. **What does cell C8 contain? How does the range appear that is included in the formula?**	
2. **View all the hidden data.**	a. **Click the row-level symbol 2.**

3. What do cells C5, C6, and C7 contain?

4. Hide all the detail data. Save and close the file My Consolidation.xls. Close all other files without saving changes.

    a. Click on the row-level symbol 1.

    b. Save the My Consolidation file. Close the file.

    c. Close all other open files without saving changes.

Use Labels In Section

If you would like to consolidate data by category, in the Use Labels In section, check the proper check box that will describe where the labels appear in the data source range. The choices are Top Row, Left Column, or both.

DISCOVERY ACTIVITY 2-4

Consolidating More Data

Data Files:

- Category Consolidation.xls

Setup:

Excel is running and no files are open.

Scenario:

You have a workbook, called Category Consolidation, that contains multiple worksheets. Each worksheet has some information on it that you would like to consolidate onto one sheet. The only problem is that these worksheets were not created with the same template. They contain similar information, but the data is located in all different areas. You will consolidate the similar information on the Consolidated worksheet within the workbook. When you are finished, you will save the file as My Category Consolidation.

1. Open the file Category Consolidation.

2. What information on the three sheets in Category Consolidation.xls is similar, and what is different?

3. On the Consolidated worksheet, **select cell A6 and consolidate the data from columns A and B of the three worksheets, Jaen, Monder, and Hanover.** (In this activity, the Commissions column will auto-generate totals for you.)

 To bring in the unique labels of Column A, make sure to check the Left Column option under the Use Labels In section.

4. **What effect did the consolidation have on the worksheet.**

When you are finished, **save the file as** *My Category Consolidation* **and close the file.**

TOPIC C

Link Cells in Different Workbooks

You have seen how you can save time and be more efficient while working with multiple workbooks by associating data. Now you will link various cells in different workbooks.

Linking workbooks is another way to prevent you from having to open multiple workbooks and copy information between workbooks that you need. Instead, you can create links to do that for you.

Link Workbooks

When you want one workbook to use data from another workbook, you create what is called a link. You can link workbooks together by writing a formula in one workbook that refers to a value in another workbook. A reference to another workbook or to a defined name in another workbook is called an *external reference*. The workbook that contains the link to another workbook is called the *dependant workbook*. The workbook to which a formula refers is called the *source workbook*.

Link Cells in Different Workbooks

Procedure Reference: Link Workbooks

To link two workbooks together:

1. Open the workbook that you want to contain the links.

2. Open the workbooks that you want to link to.

3. Select the cell where you want to place the formula that will contain the links.

4. Begin creating a formula, selecting the cells in the other workbooks that contain the data you want to link to.

5. Press [Enter] when you are finished creating the formula.

Press the [Enter] key to enter the formula and to advance to the next row. Press [Ctrl][Enter] to enter the formula and to keep the cell selected.

ACTIVITY 2-5

Linking Cells in Multiple Workbooks

Data Files:

- Finch.xls
- Decker.xls
- Simpson.xls
- Summary.xls

Setup:

Excel is running and no files are open.

Scenario:

You want to calculate the total sales and total commission for the three sales reps using the files Finch, Decker, and Simpson. You will use the Summary workbook to add links to these workbooks and calculate these totals.

What You Do	How You Do It
1. **Open the files Summary, Finch, Decker, and Simpson**	a. **Click the Open button.**
	b. **Browse and select the files named Summary, Finch, Decker, and Simpson** with the mouse while holding down the Ctrl key.
	c. **Click Open.**
2. **What are the similarities between the Finch, Decker, Simpson, and Summary workbooks?**	
3. **Activate the Summary.xls workbook and select cell A5.** This is a simple summary worksheet that will show total sales and commissions for January. You will link this worksheet to values in the other three.	a. **Click on the Summary workbook in the task bar.**
	b. **Select cell A5.**

4. **Create a formula in cell A5 that sums cell D15 in each of the three workbooks.**

    a. **With cell A5 selected, type =.**

    b. **Choose Window→Finch and click on cell D15.**

    c. **Type +, to continue the formula.**

    d. **Choose Window→Decker, click on cell D15 and type +.**

    e. **Choose Window→Simpson, click on cell D15 and press [Ctrl][Enter].**

5. **What has happened to the contents of cell A5 on the Summary worksheet?**

    Save the file as *My Summary* and close all open files without saving changes.

 Because these workbooks are now linked, whenever you make a change to one of the workbooks, the information that is linked to them will change as well.

TOPIC D

Edit Links

Now that you have created links in your workbook, you will need to know how to edit these links. In this lesson you will edit the links.

You have created links in a worksheet, but one of the source document names has been changed. If you don't change the link, the data that is being used is not correct. For example, if you have an address book and you use it to address letters, and the name and address of someone has changed and you don't update your address book, you will be sending letters to the wrong person and they will never get the information you wanted them to.

Edit Links

Procedure Reference: Edit Links

You can redirect the links in a dependant workbook by using the Edit→Links command. To redirect the links:

1. In the Edit Links dialog box, click the Change Source button.

2. Select the name of the workbook to which you want to redirect the link.

3. Click OK to return to the Edit Links dialog box.

4.   Click OK to close it.

ACTIVITY 2-6

Changing the Source Document

Data Files:

- New Summary.xls

Setup:

Excel is running, no files are open.

Scenario:

Janet Simpson is changing her name to Janet Sandeford. Her workbook, which is likened to the New Summary workbook, has to be renamed Sandeford, instead of Simpson. This change will require you to change the link in the New Summary workbook. Once you have updated the links, you will save the file as My New Summary and close the workbook.

What You Do	How You Do It
1. Open the file Simpson.xls and resave it as *Sandeford.xls*. Close the file when you are finished and open the file New Summary.xls. The file New Summary is the same file you were using in the previous activity.	a. **Open the file Simpson.** b. **Choose File→Save As.** In the File Name text box, **type** *Sandeford* **and click Save.** c. **Close the Sandeford file and open the New Summary file.** d. **Click Update** to update the existing links. If necessary, **click Continue.**
2. Using the Edit menu, **change the source file of Simpson.xls to Sandeford.xls.**	a. **Choose Edit→Links** to display the Edit Links dialog box. The Summary workbook is still linked to the Simpson workbook, not the new workbook Sandeford. If you change the name of a source workbook when its dependant workbook is open, Excel will automatically change the link. In this case, the dependant workbook wasn't open, and the link hasn't been changed. b. **Select Simpson.** c. **Click Change Source.**

d. In the file list, **select Sandeford and click OK.** Sandeford now appears in the Source File list.

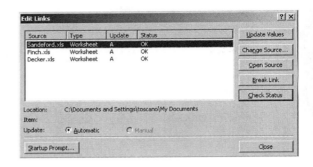

e. **Click Close.**

3. **What has happened to cell A5 in the New Summary workbook?**

Save the file as *My New Summary* and close the file.

TOPIC E

Export Excel Data as XML

In order to work with multiple data sources efficiently, you may need to export your Excel data so that it can be used in a different application. One way that you might want to export your data is using XML which will make it available on the Web as long as there is a stylesheet associated with it.

Imagine that you want to add some information to your company intranet. The person who is in charge of putting together the intranet says that you need to give him your information in XML format. You could take a few XML classes and learn how to program your data yourself, or you could just export your Excel data as XML and save yourself a lot of time and energy.

What is XML?

Extensible Markup Language (XML) is similar to HTML in that it is a method for putting structured data in a text file and contains the information necessary to multiple applications to read the text file and convert it back into the structured data by using tags.

XML tags describe the data in the text file. Unlike HTML tags though, XML tags do not include formatting or what the data should look like on screen. The following is a list of some of the features that are not retained when exported into XML from Excel.

*   Auditing tracer arrows

- Charts and other graphic objects
- Chart sheets, Macro sheets, and Dialog sheets
- Custom views
- Data consolidation references
- Drawing object layers
- Outlining
- Password settings
- Scenarios
- Shared workbook information
- User-defined function categories
- Visual Basic for Applications projects

Export Excel Data as XML Data

Procedure Reference: Export Data

To export Excel data as XML:

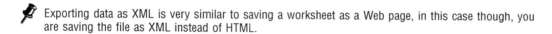 Exporting data as XML is very similar to saving a worksheet as a Web page, in this case though, you are saving the file as XML instead of HTML.

1. Open the worksheet that you want to export.

2. Choose File→Save As Web Page.

3. In the File Name Text box, type the name you want to give the XML file.

4. From the Save As Type drop-down list, select XML worksheet.

5. Click Save.

ACTIVITY 2-7

Exporting an Excel Spreadsheet as XML Data

Data Files:

- Personnel.xls

Setup:

Excel is running and no files are open.

Scenario:

You are in charge of a worksheet that contains personnel information named Personnel. You want to save the file as an XML worksheet so that it will be accessible on the intranet within your company. You will save the file in the My Documents folder and name it My Personnel.

What You Do	How You Do It
1. Using the file Personnel.xls, **start the process of saving the file as a Web page.**	a. **Open the file Personnel**, located in the My Documents folder.
	b. **Choose File→Save As Web Page.**
2. **Save the file as an XML worksheet named *My Personnel* in the My Documents folder.**	a. In the file name text box, **type *My Personnel*.**
	b. From the Save As Type drop-down list, **select XML Spreadsheet.**
	c. If necessary, from the Save In drop-down list, **select My Documents.**
	d. **Click Save.**
3. **Close the worksheet and open the XML file in Notepad** to see the XML text.	a. **Choose File→Close.**
	b. **Choose Start→Programs→Accessories→ Notepad.**
	c. In Notepad, **choose File→Open** and from the Files Of Type drop-down list, **select All Files.**
	d. **Select My Personnel and click Open.**

4. What does the file look like?

5. When you are finished, **close Notepad and all open files in Excel.**

   a. In Notepad, **choose File→Exit.**

   b. **Close any open files in Excel.**

TOPIC F

Import XML Data into Excel

Another way to work efficiently with multiple forms of data is to import the data. One of the types of data that you may find the need to import is XML. In this topic, you will import XML data into an Excel worksheet.

Imagine that your co-worker has placed some very useful information on the company's intranet site and you would like to place that information into an Excel worksheet. You could copy and paste the text in each cell, running the risk of multiple errors, incomplete data, and a pounding headache, but you would like to avoid that if possible. With Excel, you can quickly and easily import all of the XML data into your Excel worksheet.

Import XML Data into Excel

Procedure Reference: Import XML Data

You can import any properly structured XML data into Excel. To import an XML file into Excel:

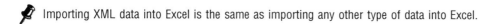 Importing XML data into Excel is the same as importing any other type of data into Excel.

1. Create a new, blank workbook in Excel.

2. Open the Select Data Source dialog box.

3. Select the XML file to import.

4. Click Open.

5. In the Import Data, select where you want the data to be inserted and click OK.

Activity 2-8

Importing XML Data into Excel

Data Files:

- Import.xml

Setup:

Excel is running and no files are open.

Scenario:

A co-worker has sent you a file called Import.xml that was posted on the company intranet site that you wanted to use in an Excel worksheet. It is an XML file and you will import this data into a new worksheet and save the worksheet as My Import.

What You Do	How You Do It
1. In a new blank workbook, import the file Import.xml into the blank worksheet.	a. In a new, blank workbook, choose Data→Import External Data→Import Data.
	b. In the Select Data Source dialog box, from the Look In drop-down list, **select My Documents.**
	c. In the file list, **select Import and click Open.**
	d. **Click OK.**
2. What do you notice about the imported file?	
Save the file as *My Import* and close the file.	

TOPIC G

Create a Web Query

In this lesson you have learned about using different sources of data in your Excel worksheet. Another source for data is the Internet and XML sources. In this topic, you will create a query that uses data from an XML source document.

Imagine that you have a worksheet that contains a formula that is dependant on the most recent stock quote for a particular stock. Now imagine that when you get this information, you open your Excel worksheet four times a day to update this information. To update this information, you need to go to a Web site, copy the stock information, and then paste it into your worksheet. All of this needs to be done regularly so that you have the most up-to-date information. Now, imagine that you could get this updated information at the click of a button. Well, you can by creating a Web query.

Create a Web Query

Procedure Reference: Create a Web Query

To create a Web query:

1. Select the cell in which you want the query data to be placed.

2. Choose Data→Import External Data→New Web Query.

3. In the New Web Query dialog box, in the address bar, type in the location of the Web data you want to query.

4. Select the tables you want to query.

5. If you are importing XML data, click the Options button and select Full HTML Formatting and click OK.

6. Click Import.

ACTIVITY 2-9

Creating a Web Query using XML Data

Data Files:

*   Available Commissions.xls

*   Realestate.xml

Setup:

Excel is running and no files are open.

Scenario:

You are responsible for keeping track of the commissions that are available on the houses that are for sale in your department in a file called Available Commissions. You have found yourself constantly importing the house listing information (kept in a file called Realestate) into your worksheet since this information changes on a daily basis. Now you want to create a query to that XML file so that the listing information is updated daily. You will name the file that contains the query My Available Commissions and then close the file when you are finished.

What You Do	How You Do It
1. In the file Available Commissions, **create a Web query from the XML file Realestate.xml located in the XML Data folder on your C drive. Use full HTML formatting and place the query data in cell A3 so that the formulas will work.**	a. **Open the file Available Commissions.** Observe that the formulas for calculating the commissions are already set up.
	b. **Select cell A3.**
	c. **Choose Data→Import External Data→ New Web Query.**
	d. The file you will be querying is on your hard drive so in the address bar **type c:/xml data/realestate.xml**.
	e. **Click Go.**

f. Select the table that lists the four homes for sale.

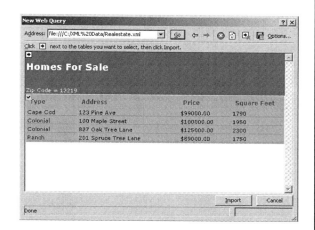

g. In the New Web Query window toolbar, **click Options** and under Formatting **select Full HTML Formatting. Click OK.**

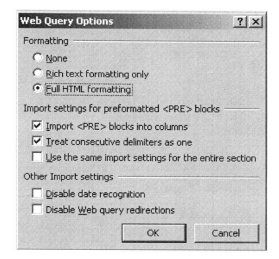

h. **Click Import and click OK.**

---

2. **Update the queried data and save the file as *My Available Commissions*. Close the file.**

a. On the External Data toolbar, **click the Refresh Data button.** If the source of the queried data has changed, the new data will be shown.

b. **Save the file as *My Available Commissions*.**

c. **Close the file.**

Lesson 2: Working with Multiple Data Sources

Lesson 2 Follow-up

In this lesson, you learned how to create a workspace containing multiple workbooks and consolidate your data from multiple workbooks. You also learned how to link cells from different workbooks and then edit those links. You exported Excel data as XML and imported XML data into Excel. Finally you created a Web query using existing XML data.

1. When you are working with multiple sources of data back at the office, which of the techniques you learned in this lesson will be most applicable to you?

2. How will you use your new understanding of working with multiple sources of data? Which of your projects that you are currently working on could benefit from your new knowledge?

LESSON 3
Collaborating with Others Using Workbooks

Lesson Time
50 minutes to 60 minutes

Lesson Objectives:

In this lesson, you will collaborate with other Excel users by protecting your workbook, sharing your workbook, setting revision tracking, merging multiple copies of the same workbook, and tracking changes.

You will:

- Protect your worksheets.
- Protect the structure of your workbook by protecting your workbook.
- Share your workbook.
- Set revision tracking.
- Merge four copies of the same workbook.
- Track the changes in your merged workbook.

LESSON 3

Introduction

You know how to work with workbooks on your own, but now it is time to learn how to work with workbooks with other Excel users. In this lesson, you will protect your worksheet and workbook before you share your workbook, set revision tracking, merge the workbooks, and track changes to the workbook.

Imagine that you have a workbook that you would like some of your co-workers to look at and give you feedback on. You could email the workbook to each of them. The problem with this is that each one will have their own edits and they could make changes to things that you didn't want them to change (like a logo that has to be a particular size, or a formula that shouldn't be changed or it will affect the entire worksheet), not to mention wasting valuable network space by sending out all those emails with attachments. Wouldn't it be nice if you could just place the file somewhere and have everyone make changes to that one file, and ensure that the things you don't want changed are protected? Well, in this lesson you will learn how to easily and efficiently collaborate with others using your workbook.

TOPIC A

Protect your Worksheets

Before you begin your collaboration with other Excel users, you want to protect your worksheet. In this topic, you will protect your worksheet by locking and unlocking cells and then adding worksheet protection.

You want to share your worksheet with some co-workers. You have asked them for general comments and some possible grammar or minor changes. You would like to make parts of your worksheet safe from modification. With Excel, you can protect all of those things that you don't want your co-workers to change.

What Can Be Protected?

You can protect a worksheet to prevent other users from changing the contents. When you enable worksheet protection, you can choose which elements of the worksheet you want other users to be able to edit, protecting those which you do not want them to be able to edit. By selecting the option in the Protect Sheet dialog box, you are enabling other users to edit the selected option. The following list describes the options you have when protecting your worksheet.

When you are protecting a worksheet, you can choose whether or not to allow other users to:

- Select locked or unlocked cells
- Format cells, columns, and rows
- Insert columns, rows, and hyperlinks
- Delete columns or rows
- Sort
- Use AutoFilter and PivotTable reports
- Edit objects and scenarios

Protect Your Worksheets

Procedure Reference: Protect Your Worksheets

After you complete a worksheet, you can protect the entire worksheet, or specific cells within the worksheet, so that the worksheet or cell contents cannot be changed. For example, you might want to protect cells that contain formulas. When someone tries to enter data into a protected cell, a message immediately appears, and the data cannot be entered. To add protection to your worksheet:

1. Unlock all cells that you don't want protected.

2. Open the Protect Sheet dialog box.

3. Verify that Protect Worksheet And Contents Of Locked Cells is selected.

4. Select the options that you want users to be able to do when the worksheet is protected.

5. Click OK.

 To unprotect your worksheet, choose Tools→Protection→Unprotect Sheet.

Lock and Unlock Cells

Protecting a range of cells involves two processes: locking and protecting. By default, all cells are locked. Therefore, you must unlock the cells that you do not want protected. After you have unlocked selected cells, you can enable sheet protection. Before sheet protection is enabled, you can still change the contents of a cell, regardless of whether it is locked or not.

ACTIVITY 3-1

Protecting Your Worksheet

Data Files:

*   Display.xls

Setup:

Excel is running and no files are open.

Scenario:

Before you begin your collaboration with other Excel users on your worksheet (Display), you want to add protection to the formulas and the graphic objects in the worksheet. When you are finished, you will save the file as My Display.

LESSON 3

What You Do	How You Do It
1. In the file Display.xls, **unlock all the cells, except for the formulas.**	a. **Open the file Display.**
	b. **Choose Edit→Go To.**
	c. **Click Special** to display the Go To Special dialog box.

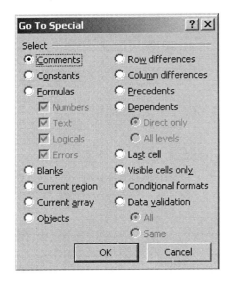

	d. **Select Constants.** You will unlock all the cells that don't contain formulas.
	e. **Click OK.** All the cells that contain constants are selected.
2. On the Protection tab of the Format Cells dialog box, **remove the locks from the cells containing constants.**	a. **Choose Format→Cells.**
	b. **Select the Protection tab.**
	c. **Uncheck Locked to remove the locks from the cells containing constants.**
	d. **Click OK and deselect the selected cells.**

3. Protect the worksheet and the contents of the locked cells and allow all users to select locked cells, select unlocked cells, sort, use AutoFilter, and use PivotTable Reports.

   In the Protect Sheet dialog box, you can also add a password that users will need to know in order to access the worksheet. Be careful though—if you forget the password, you will not be able to get into your worksheet.

   a. Choose Tools→Protection→Protect Sheet.

      To unprotect your worksheet, choose Tools→ Protection→Unprotect Sheet.

   b. Verify that Protect Worksheet And Contents Of Locked Cells is selected.

   c. In the Allow All Users Of This Worksheet To list box, verify that Select Locked Cells and Select Unlocked Cells are selected.

   d. Scroll down and select Sort, Use AutoFilter, and Use PivotTable reports.

   e. Click OK.

4. Save the file as *My Display* and try to make changes to one of the formulas and resize the graphic object.

   a. Save the file as *My Display*.

   b. Select cell F10. You can see the contents of the cell which is a formula.

   c. Type *15*. Click OK.

5. What happens when you try to make a change to the formula? What happens when you try to resize the graphic object?

TOPIC B

Protect Your Workbook

Now that you know how to protect the contents of a worksheet, you will want to know how to protect the structure and windows within a workbook before using it to collaborate with others. In this topic, you will protect the structure and windows within your workbook.

You have sent the protected workbook to your co-workers to suggest and make some changes. You aren't worried about them changing your formulas, but you are worried about the structure and that they might feel the need to re-arrange the order of the worksheets within the workbook. Well, don't worry, you can protect that as well.

Protect Your Workbook

Procedure Reference: Protect Your Workbook

To protect your workbook:

1. Open the Protect Workbook dialog box.

2. Select the appropriate options.

3. Enter a password, if desired.

4. Click OK.

ACTIVITY 3-2

Protecting Your Workbook

Setup:
The file My Display.xls is open.

Scenario:
You have protected the cells and parts of your worksheet that you don't want others to edit. Now you want to protect the structure of your workbook so that the worksheets within your workbook cannot be moved around.

What You Do	How You Do It
1. Protect the workbook structure.	a. Choose Tools→Protection→Protect Workbook to open the Protect Workbook dialog box.

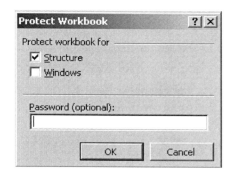

	b. Verify that Structure is selected and click OK.
	You can also add a password to the workbook, but remember if you forget your password, you can't unprotect the workbook.
2. Save the file and try to move the worksheet around.	a. Save the file.
	b. Try to move the Sheet2 tab before the Sheet1 tab.

3. What happens when you try to change the position of the worksheets?

Save and close the file.

TOPIC C

Share Your Workbook

Now that you have protected your data and the structure of your workbook, you are ready to share the workbook. In this topic, you will share your workbook with multiple users.

So you want your co-workers to look at your worksheet and make some suggestions. You could send them each the file in an email, but then you would have many copies of the file floating around and they could get mixed up. If you place it on your network as is, then only one of them can edit it at a time. Well, Excel 2002 offers you a solution. You can share your workbook with multiple users.

Collaboration Process

When you are collaborating with others to share Excel workbooks, you will always follow the same guidelines. Below is the collaboration process.

1. First, you need to protect the parts of your worksheet that you don't want anyone to be able to make changes to.

2. Save your workbook as a shared workbook, which will allow multiple users to make changes to the file at the same time.

3. Have others makes changes to the worksheet.

4. You review the changes made by others and if you choose to, you can incorporate those changes into your worksheet.

What is a Shared Workbook?

A shared workbook is a workbook that is set up and saved to allow multiple users on the same network to view, edit, and save the workbook at the same time. Each person who saves the workbook can see the changes that have been made by other users.

Share Your Workbook

Procedure Reference: Share Workbooks

To share a workbook:

1. Open the workbook you want to share.

2. Open the Share Workbook dialog box.

3. Verify that the Editing tab is selected.

4. Select the Allow Changes By More Than One User At The Same Time option.

5. On the Advanced tab, under Track Changes, verify that Keep Change History For is selected.

6. In the Days text box, enter the amount of days that you want to maintain the change history.

7. Click OK twice.

8. Save the workbook on a network location where other users can access it.

ACTIVITY 3-3

Sharing Your Workbook

Data Files:

• Shared.xls

Setup:

Students need to be split into groups of three or four. A network needs to be available for saving the shared workbook file on it.

Scenario:

You have a workbook that contains department numbers from four different departments called Shared. One of the departments is your own, so you can update those numbers yourself. The other three departments need to be updated by some of your co-workers (the other members of your group). In order for them to do this you want to make your workbook a shared workbook and save it on a designated location on a network. You will save the file using your first initial and last name as the file name.

LESSON 3

What You Do	How You Do It
1. Save the file Shared.xls as a shared workbook that allows multiple users to update it at once.	a. **Open the file Shared.**
	b. **Choose Tools→Share Workbook.**
	c. If necessary, in the Shared Workbook dialog box, on the Editing tab, **check Allow Changes By More Than One User At The Same Time.**
	d. **Activate the Advanced tab.**
	e. In the Track Changes section, **change the number of days to Keep Change History For to *15*.**
	f. **Click OK.**
	g. If you are prompted to continue, **click OK.**
2. Save the file in a location on your network and name it using your first initial and last name as the file name.	a. **Choose File→Save As.**
	b. **Navigate to the specified network location.**
	c. In the File Name text box, **type your first initial and last name.**
	d. **Click Save.** You have now created a shared workbook.

TOPIC D

Set Revision Tracking

Now that you know how to share your workbook, you want to set the revision tracking so you can take full advantage of the collaboration capabilities of Excel. In this topic, you will set the revision tracking so that any changes made by other users will be tracked.

So you have shared your workbook. Others can now make changes to the workbook. You are worried though that when all those co-workers make their changes, you won't have any idea who made what changes. For example, you want to be sure to implement the changes that your boss suggested, but the changes that your peers suggested may not be as valuable to you. In order for you to know who is making what changes, you need to set revision tracking. You will then be able to go through and decide which revisions to implement and which revisions to reject.

Set Revision Tracking

Procedure Reference: Track Changes

After you create a workbook, you will want to turn on the revision tracking so that after you merge the changed workbooks, you can track the changes made by all the users. To turn on the revision tracking:

1. Verify that the shared workbook is open.

2. Open the Protect Shared Workbook dialog box.

3. Select Sharing With Track Changes.

4. Click OK.

ACTIVITY 3-4

Setting Revision Tracking

Setup:

The file that is named with your first initial and last name is open.

Scenario:

Now that you have created your shared workbook, you want to set the revision tracking so that when others make changes to it, you can track who made what changes. You will set the revision tracking in your workbook and save the file.

What You Do	How You Do It
1. **Turn on revision tracking in your shared workbook.**	a. With your shared workbook open, **choose Tools→Protection→Protect Shared Workbook.**
	b. In the Protect Shared Workbook dialog box, **check Sharing With Track Changes.**
	c. **Click OK.**
2. **Save and close the file.**	a. **Save the file.**
	b. **Close the file.**

ACTIVITY 3-5

Making Changes to a Shared Workbook

Setup:

Students should be divided into groups of three or four. Each student should have a paper tent on their computer that has their first initial and last name on it so you know what that person's shared file name is. Within your group, assign each person as Student A, Student B, Student C, and Student D. Make a note of which student you are on your name tent.

Scenario:

Now that you have shared your workbook, you are going to make some changes to it. You and your partners (A, B, C, and D) are going to be making changes to each others' workbooks and saving changes by adding your individual letters to the end of the file name.

What You Do	How You Do It

 At one point in this activity, you will be opening your own workbook and making changes to it. Save it in the same way you are saving the other workbooks.

1. **Make changes to student A's work-book, filling in numbers in your column. Save the file with a unique name and close the file.**

    The numbers that you fill in in the worksheets of your partners can be any number.

   a. **Open Student A's shared workbook.**

   b. **Fill in numbers in your column, depend-ing on whether you are student A, B, C, or D.**

   c. **Choose File→Save As. Save with a new file name by adding your student letter to the end of the file name.**

   d. **Close the file.**

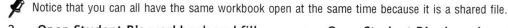 Notice that you can all have the same workbook open at the same time because it is a shared file.

2. **Open Student B's workbook and fill in your numbers in your column. Save the file with a unique name. Close the file when you are finished.**

   a. **Open Student B's shared workbook.**

   b. **Fill in numbers in your column, depend-ing on whether you are student A, B, C, or D.**

   c. **Choose File→Save As. Save with a new file name by adding your student letter to the end of the file name.**

   d. **Close the file.**

3. Make changes to students C and D's workbooks and save them with unique names.

   a. Open Student C's shared workbook.

   b. Fill in numbers in your column, depending on whether you are student A, B, C, or D.

   c. Choose File→Save As. Save with a new file name by adding your student letter to the end of the file name.

   d. Close the file.

   e. Open Student D's shared workbook.

   f. Fill in numbers in your column, depending on whether you are student A, B, C, or D.

   g. Choose File→Save As. Save with a new file name by adding your student letter to the end of the file name.

   h. Close the file.

TOPIC E

Merge Workbooks

You have shared your workbook and set revision tracking so all the revisions that people have made to that shared workbook are tracked. Now that you have completed all of this, you are ready to look at the changes in one workbook. In this topic, you will merge all of the workbooks that contain revisions from the shared workbook.

You have shared your workbook with your manager and co-workers. You have also set the revision tracking so that the changes they made would be tracked. Now, you want to combine all of those marks into one workbook. You are afraid that you will have to open each copy of the workbook and write down the changes that each person suggested. This could take hours or even days depending on how many people have seen the workbook and how many changes they have made. Well, Excel can do this for you. In one simple procedure, you can merge all of those revisions into one workbook that is easy to work with.

Merge Workbooks

Procedure Reference: Merge Workbooks

To merge changes from multiple copies of a shared workbook:

1. Open the copy of the shared workbook where you want to merge the changes from the copies.

2. Open the Select Files To Merge Into Current Workbook dialog box.

3. Click OK to save the current file.

4. Select all the files that have changes to be merged.

5. Click OK.

6. Save the merged file.

ACTIVITY 3-6

Merging Workbooks

Setup:

Excel is running and no files are open.

Scenario:

You now have up to five different copies of your worksheet. One is your original and the other four are the ones that your partners made changes to. Now, you will merge the four workbooks, that your partners saved their changes to, into your original workbook.

What You Do	How You Do It
1. Open your original file that you created as a shared workbook.	a. Choose File→Open.
	b. Navigate to the location where you were instructed to save your shared workbook.
	c. Select your original shared workbook and click Open.

2. **Merge the workbook with the copies of the workbooks that your partners created.**

   a. **Choose Tools→Compare And Merge Workbooks.**

   b. From the file list, **select the workbooks that your partners and you created from your original file.**

   c. **Click OK.** The data from the other files has merged into your original file.

TOPIC F

Track Changes

Now that you have merged all the copies of your workbooks together, you want to implement some of the changes that were suggested. In this topic, you will track changes in the merged workbook by accepting and rejecting the changes.

So you have a workbook that is full of changes made by other people. Suppose you don't want to make all of the changes that everyone suggests. Suppose you only want to implement the changes that your boss made. Well, you can do this by accepting or rejecting tracked changes.

Track Changes

Procedure Reference: Track Changes

After you merge the changes from a shared workbook, you can accept or reject those changes. You can review each change individually and accept or reject that change. You can also accept or reject all the changes at one time. To track the changes made to your shared workbook:

1. Verify that the merged workbook is open and appears in the worksheet window.

2. Open the Select Changes To Accept Or Reject dialog box.

3. If Excel prompts you to save the workbook, click OK.

4. Select the change you want to review.

    • To review changes made by another user, select Who and click the user in the Who box.

    • To review changes made by all users, deselect the Who option.

    • To review changes to a specific area on a worksheet, select Where and enter a reference to the area.

    • To review changes to the entire workbook, deselect Where.

5. Click OK.

6. Either accept or reject the change.

- To accept a change, click Accept.
- To reject a change, click Reject.
- You can also click Accept All or Reject All to accept or reject all remaining changes.

7. Save the file when you have finished.

ACTIVITY 3-7

Tracking Changes

Scenario:

Now that you have merged your workbooks together, you want to see who made what changes and determine whether you want to use those changes. You will review the changes in your merged workbook so that all the changes have been either accepted or rejected. When you are finished, you will save the file in the My Documents folder as My Merged Workbook.

What You Do	How You Do It
1. Turn on the Track Changes feature to accept and reject all changes that have not yet been reviewed.	a. Choose Tools→Track Changes→Accept Or Reject Changes. b. In the Select Changes To Accept Or Reject dialog box, **verify that the When box is checked and that Not Yet Reviewed is displayed in the When text box.** c. **Click OK.** 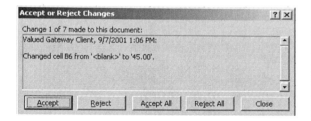
2. Accept the first two changes individually, then accept all the changes at once.	a. **Click the Accept button.** Excel moves to the next cell and prompts you to accept or reject that change. **Click Accept.**

3. What information is displayed in the Accept Or Reject Changes window when it locates a change?

Click Accept All to accept all the changes made to the worksheet.

4. Save the file as *My Merged Workbook* and close the file.

a. Save the file as *My Merged Workbook*.

b. Save and close the file.

Lesson 3 Follow-up

In this lesson, you collaborated with other Excel users by protecting your workbook, sharing your workbook, setting revision tracking, merging multiple copies of the same workbook, and tracking changes.

1. How can you use the sharing workbooks feature back at your office?

2. What things do you think you will want to protect the most in your workbooks before you share them?

LESSON 4
Enhancing Your Worksheet Using Charts

Lesson Time
40 minutes

Lesson Objectives:

In this lesson, you will chart non-adjacent data, modify chart items, and create a trendline.

You will:

* Chart non-adjacent data.
* Modify chart items.
* Add a trend line to your chart.

Introduction

You already know how to create basic charts and use charts to graphically represent your data. In this lesson, you will learn more about using charts to enhance your worksheet. You will chart non-adjacent data, modify more chart items, and create a trend line in your chart.

Imagine that you are using a more complex chart with more complex data and want to know how to create a chart using non-adjacent data. When you are working with complex data and charts, it is useful to know how to make changes to chart items to make your graphical representations of the data more visually appealing and possibly make the chart easier to read.

TOPIC A

Chart Non-adjacent Data

You know how to chart data that is adjacent, but you need to know how to chart data that is non-adjacent. In this topic, you will chart non-adjacent data.

Imagine that you want to chart some data, but the data isn't positioned next to each other in the worksheet. Does this mean this data can't be charted? Of course not. You can chart non-adjacent data in Excel quickly and easily, just as you chart adjacent data.

Chart Non-adjacent Worksheet Data

Procedure Reference: Chart Non-adjacent Data

To create a chart from non-adjacent data:

1. Select the first range of data.

2. Press [Ctrl].

3. Select the second range of data.

4. Click the Chart Wizard button to run the chart wizard and chart the data.

ACTIVITY 4-1

Chart Non-adjacent Worksheet Data

Data Files:

- Qtr Sales.xls

Setup:

Excel is running and no files are open.

Scenario:

You have a worksheet (Qtr Sales) that contains information on four quarters. You want to create a column chart based on the Quarter 1 and Quarter 4 sales numbers. Once you have done this you will save the file as My Qtr Sales and close the file.

What You Do	How You Do It
1. In the file Qtr Sales.xls, **select the data for the Quarter 1 and 4 sales.**	a. **Open the file Qtr Sales.**
	b. **Select the range A5:B9.**
	c. **Press [Ctrl].**
	d. **Select the range E5:E9. Release [Ctrl].**
2. **Run the Chart wizard and create a column chart entitled** *Qtr 1 and 4 Sales*. **Create a new chart sheet for this chart. Save the file as** *My Qtr Sales* **and close it.**	a. **Click the Chart Wizard** 📊 **button.**
	b. **Verify that the Column is selected. Click Next.**
	c. In the second screen of the wizard, **click Next.**
	d. On the Titles tab, in the Chart Title text box, **type** *Qtr 1 and 4 Sales*. **Click Next.**

e. In the last screen of the wizard, **select As New Sheet and click Finish.**

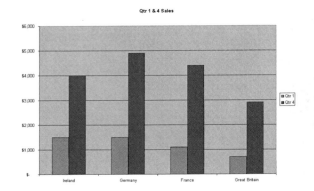

f. **Save the file as** *My Qtr Sales.*

g. **Close the file.**

TOPIC B

Modify Chart Items

You have already modified some chart items like chart titles and legends, but there are many more chart items that can be modified. In this topic, you will look at and modify some advanced chart items.

You know how to modify your chart title. But, what happens if you have a chart with a negative number and you want to change the direction of an axis? Or, what if you want to add another axis to your chart? Once you learn how to modify chart items, you can modify any chart item you wish and see all of the formatting options that are available.

Modify Chart Items

Procedure Reference: Modify Chart Items

To modify chart items:

1. Right-click on the chart item you want to modify.

2. Select the Format object menu choice.

3. In the Format dialog box, make the desired changes.

4. Click OK.

ACTIVITY 4-2

Format Chart Items

Data Files:

- Pottery Performance.xls

Setup:

Excel is running and no files are open.

Scenario:

You are working in a workbook called Pottery Performance. On the Scatter Plot graph, you want to modify the data series so that the X error bar displays both plus and minus numbers. You also want to change the color of the data series. You also want to format the axis so that there are no major tick marks and the tick mark labels are high. Once you have done this, you will save the file as My Pottery Performance. When you are finished, your graph should look like Figure 4-1.

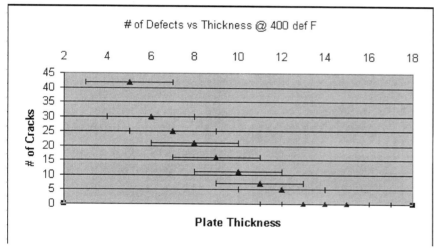

Figure 4-1: *Scatter plot at the completion of the activity.*

LESSON 4

What You Do	How You Do It
1. On the scatter plot, **modify the data series so that the X error bar displays both plus and minus numbers. Change the data marker to triangles.**	a. **Open the file Pottery Performance.**
	b. **Click on the Scatter Plot sheet tab.**
	c. Select the data series.
	d. **Right-click on the data series and choose Format Data Series.**
	e. Select the X Error Bars tab.
	f. Under display, **select Both.**
	g. **Select the Patterns tab.**
	h. In the Marker section, from the Style drop-down list, **select the triangle.**
	i. **Click OK.**
2. Format the axis so that the major tick marks appear inside and the tick mark labels are low. Save the file as *My Pottery Performance.*	a. **Right-click on the Value(X) Axis.**
	b. **Choose Format Axis.**
	c. On the Patterns tab, under Major Tick Mark Type, **select None.**
	d. In the Tick Mark Labels section, **select High.**
	e. **Click OK.**
	f. **Save the file as *My Pottery Performance.***

ACTIVITY 4-3

Formatting More Chart Items

Scenario:

You now want to work on the surface chart in the Pottery Performance file. First you will change the location of the chart by placing it on its own chart sheet. Then, you will format the floor of the surface chart by making it a lighter gray. Finally, you will adjust the 3-D View of the surface chart. When you are finished, save the file. Your chart should look similar to Figure 4-2 when you are finished.

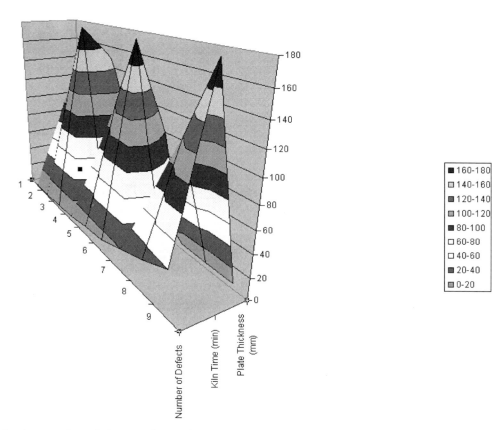

Figure 4-2: *A sample of the surface chart after the activity is complete.*

What You Do	How You Do It
1. Change the location of the surface chart by putting it on its own chart sheet.	a. Select the Surface Chart tab.
	b. Select the chart.
	c. Right-click on the chart area and choose Location.
	d. Select As New Sheet and click OK.

2. Change the Surface Chart floor to a lighter shade of gray.

a. Right-click on the surface chart floor.

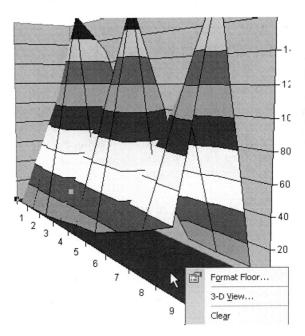

b. Choose Format Floor.

c. Select a light shade of gray and click OK.

3. Adjust the 3-D view of the surface chart to your liking. **Save the file as** *My Pottery Performance*.

a. Right-click anywhere on the chart.

b. **Choose 3-D View.**

c. In the 3-D View dialog box, **change the 3-D view** however you would like it to appear. **Click OK.**

TOPIC C

Create a Trendline

You know how to use data to create a chart. Now you will use a trendline to help interpret the data on that chart.

What good is data if you can't interpret it? When you chart data, you are creating a graphic representation of that data. In order for you to be able to use that chart effectively, you need to understand and interpret the data and its implications. You can do this using a trendline.

What is a Trendline?

A trendline is a graphic representation of trends in a data series. Trendlines are used to study predictions in data.

Add a Trendline to your Chart

Procedure Reference: Add Trendlines

To add a trendline to a chart:

1. Select the data series you want to add a trendline to.

2. Open the Add Trendline dialog box.

3. Select the type of trendline you want.

4. Determine how far ahead or behind you want to forecast in the Forecast text box.

5. Click OK.

ACTIVITY 4-4

Adding a Trendline to Your Chart

Setup:

The file My Pottery Performance.xls is open.

Scenario:

Your boss has given you a scatter plot chart to use for your reports. You want to better understand this data and what it implies, so, you will add a linear trendline and forecast it forward 2 units to the scatter plot (refer to Figure 4-3). When you are finished, you will save and close the file.

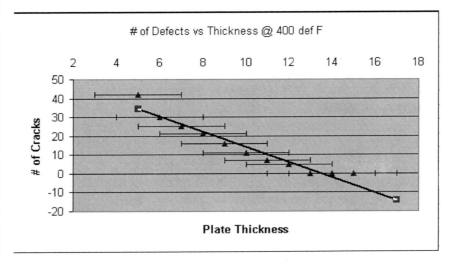

Figure 4-3: *The scatter plot with a trendline.*

What You Do	How You Do It
1. **Open the Add Trendline dialog box for the scatter plot data series.**	a. **Select the Scatter Plot sheet tab.**
	b. **Select the data series.**
	c. **Choose Chart→Add Trendline.**

2. Add a linear trendline that will forecast the data forward 2 units. Save and close the file when you are finished.

    a. On the Type tab, if necessary, **select Linear.**

    b. **Select the Options tab.**

    c. In the Forecast section, in the Forward text box, **select the text and type 2.**

    d. **Click OK.**

    e. **Save and close the file.**

Lesson 4 Follow-up

In this lesson you charted non-adjacent data. Then, you modified different chart items. Finally, you created a trendline.

1. **What are the chart items that you think you will modify the most when you are back at the office and using your own worksheets?**

2. **Do you think that you will use the trendline feature? What data of yours will you use it with?**

LESSON 5
Using Graphic Objects to Enhance your Worksheets

Lesson Time
50 minutes to 60 minutes

Lesson Objectives:

In this lesson, you will use multiple graphic objects to enhance your worksheet.

You will:

- Create graphic objects.
- Move, resize, and copy existing graphic objects.
- Change the order of your graphic objects.
- Group multiple graphic objects.
- Format graphic objects.
- Insert clip art.
- Modify clip art.

LESSON 5

Introduction

You already know how to enhance your worksheets using charts, now you will learn how to use other graphic objects to enhance your worksheets.

There can be more to Excel worksheets than just numbers. Imagine that you have a worksheet that you need to use for a presentation. You can add arrows to point out figures that you are particularly proud of. You can also add clip art and other objects to make your worksheet more visually appealing.

TOPIC A

Create Graphic Objects

The first step to using graphic objects to enhance your worksheet is to create the graphic objects. Once you have done that, you can manipulate them to best fit your needs. In this topic, you will create multiple graphic objects.

In order to begin enhancing your worksheet with graphics, you need to first create those graphic objects.

The Drawing Toolbar

The Drawing toolbar contains all the tools you need to create your graphic objects. Use Figure 5-1 and the following table to identify the tools on the drawing toolbar.

Figure 5-1: *The Drawing toolbar*.

Button	Description
Draw ▾	The Draw drop-down button allows you to change the position of your graphic object, group and ungroup multiple objects, and change the AutoShape of an AutoShape graphic object.
AutoShapes ▾	The AutoShape drop-down button allows you to create an autoshape object. The categories of autoshapes include lines, arrows, basic shapes, block arrows, flowchart, stars and banners, and callouts. You can also choose from a number of clip art autoshapes that can be accessed by clicking on More AutoShapes.
\	The Line button allows you to draw a line anywhere on the worksheet.
↘	The Arrow button allows you to draw a simple arrow anywhere on the worksheet.

Button	Description
	The Rectangle button allows you to draw a rectangle or square anywhere on the worksheet.
	The Ellipse button allows you to draw a circle or ellipse anywhere on your worksheet.
	The Text Box button allows you to draw a text box in which you can type and format text.
	The Insert WordArt button allows you to create a WordArt shape.
	The Insert Diagram Or Organizational Chart button allows you to insert a diagram or create an organizational chart.
	The Insert Clip Art button displays the Insert Clip Art task pane and allows you to insert a clip art object from your computer or from the Web.
	The Insert Picture From File button allows you to insert an existing picture file into your worksheet. For example, a company logo.
	The Fill Color button allows you to change the fill color of all graphic objects.
	The Line Color button allows you to choose the color of the lines in your selected graphic object.
	The Font Color button allows you to change the font color of text within a text box.
	The Line Style button allows you to change the style and weight of the lines in the selected graphic object.
	The Dash Style button allows you to change the style of a line to a dashed line with multiple options for dashed line style.
	The Arrow style button allows you to change the style of the arrow that is selected.
	The Shadow Style button allows you to add a shadow to a graphic object and then change the kind of shadow that is applied.
	The 3-D Style button allows you to add and change the style of 3-D effects on a graphic object.

What are Graphic Objects?

Definition:

A graphic object is an item that you add to a worksheet that is either drawn or inserted. The buttons on the Drawing toolbar allow you to create lines, arrows, shapes, and text boxes. All of these items are not part of the Excel data and are considered graphic objects.

Example:

For example, if you insert an electronic copy of your company logo into your worksheet, then that logo is a graphic object.

Create Graphic Objects

Procedure Reference: Create Graphic Objects

To create a graphic object using the drawing toolbar:

1. Click the appropriate drawing button.

2. Place the mouse pointer where you want to begin drawing the object.

3. Drag the mouse pointer in the workbook or chart sheet until the object is the desired shape and size.

ACTIVITY 5-1

Creating Graphic Objects

Data Files:

*   Objects.xls

Setup:

Excel is running and no files are open.

Scenario:

You have a worksheet named Objects.xls that you want to use for a presentation. Before you show this workbook to your co-workers, you want to highlight the fact that the Germany department had a great year. First you will experiment with the drawing toolbar a little, adding various graphic objects and deleting them. When you have finished exploring, you will add a text box that reads"Germany did great this year!" and draw an arrow from the text box to the Germany Qtr total in the chart data. You will further highlight the Germany total by placing a circle object around the total number in the chart data. When you are finished, you will save the file as My Objects. Your worksheet should look like the example in Figure 5-2.

	A	B	C	D	E	F	G	H	I	J	K	L
1												
2		Books and Beyond, Inc.										
3		Quarterly Sales Report										
4												
5	Location	Qtr 1	Qtr 2	Qtr 3	Qtr 4	Total			Germany did great this year!			
6	Australia	$1,500	$1,500	$3,000	$ 4,000	$10,000						
7	Germany	$1,500	$1,800	$2,600	$ 4,900	$10,800						
8	Canada	$1,100	$1,300	$1,800	$ 4,400	$ 8,600						
9	Great Britain	$ 700	$1,800	$1,600	$ 2,900	$ 7,000						
10	Quarter Total	$4,800	$6,400	$9,000	$16,200	$36,400						
11												

Figure 5-2: *Objects.xls after the completion of the activity.*

What You Do	How You Do It
1. In the file Objects.xls **display the drawing toolbar and experiment by adding and deleting several graphic objects.**	a. **Open the file Objects.**
	b. If necessary, **click the Drawing button on the Standard toolbar to display the Drawing toolbar.**
	c. On the Drawing toolbar, **click the Line button.**
	d. **Place the mouse pointer in a blank area of the worksheet. Drag and release the mouse pointer in the worksheet to create a line.**
	e. Using the Arrow button, **create an arrow line the same way you created the plain line.**
	f. **Place the mouse pointer on either of the arrow's selection handle.** The mouse pointer changes to a double-sided arrow. **Drag toward the opposite selection handle to make the arrow smaller.**
	g. With the arrow object selected, **press [Delete].**
	h. **Select the line object and press [Delete].**

2. Create a text box object next to the chart data that contains the text "Germany did great this year!" Then, create an arrow that goes from the text box to the Germany total number in the chart data.

   a. On the Drawing toolbar, **click the Text Box button.**

   b. Place the mouse pointer on cell J4. Press and hold the mouse button and drag down to cell L7.

   c. Type *Germany did great this year!* Click on any cell to deselect the text box.

   d. Click the Arrow button on the Drawing toolbar.

   e. Draw an arrow from the text box to the Germany total in the chart data. Use Figure 5-2 as a guide.

3. Draw a circle around the Germany total in the chart data. Set the fill to No Fill. When you are finished, save the file as *My Objects*.

   a. Click the Oval button on the Drawing toolbar.

   b. Place the mouse pointer at the top left corner of cell F7. Drag down and to the right until the entire number is in the oval. Release the mouse button.

   c. Click the Fill Color drop-down arrow and select No Fill.

   d. Save the file as *My Objects*.

TOPIC B

Resize, Move, and Copy Graphic Objects

Now that you know how to create graphic objects, you will want to work with them. Specifically, you will want to resize, move, and copy graphic objects. In this topic, you will resize the graphic objects, copy them, and finally move them.

So you have created your graphic objects. What happens if that object is too big? Do you have to delete it and start from scratch? What if it is in the wrong position or you want to have another of the same graphic? Well, rather than creating all new graphic objects to solve these problems, you can resize, move, and copy existing graphic objects, allowing you to work more efficiently and effectively with graphic objects.

Resize, Move, and Copy Graphic Objects

Procedure Reference: Resize a Graphic Object

To resize a graphic object:

1. Select the object you want to resize.

2. Select the sizing handles.

3. Drag in the direction you want to resize the object.

Procedure Reference: Move a Graphic Object

To move a graphic object:

1. Select the object you want to move.

2. Press and hold the mouse button.

3. Drag the object to a new location.

4. Release the mouse button.

Procedure Reference: Copy a Graphic Object

To copy a graphic object:

1. Select the object you want to copy.

2. Press the [Ctrl] key.

3. Drag the object to the location you want the copied object to be placed.

4. Release the mouse button, and then the [Ctrl] key.

> Another way to copy a graphic object is to select the object you want to copy, click the Copy button and then click the Paste button. You can then move the new graphic item to its new location.

ACTIVITY 5-2

Resize, Move, and Copy your Graphic Objects

Setup:

The file My Objects.xls is open.

Scenario:

You now have your graphic objects inserted into your My Objects file, but, you want to make a few changes to these objects. First, you want to resize the text box so that it fits the text. Then, you want to move the text box so that it is closer to the chart data. Next, you want to resize the existing arrow to better fit the new location of the text box. Finally, you want to copy the existing arrow, resize and move it so that it is pointing from the text box to the Germany pie slice on the chart. You will use Figure 5-3 as a guide. When you are finished, save the file.

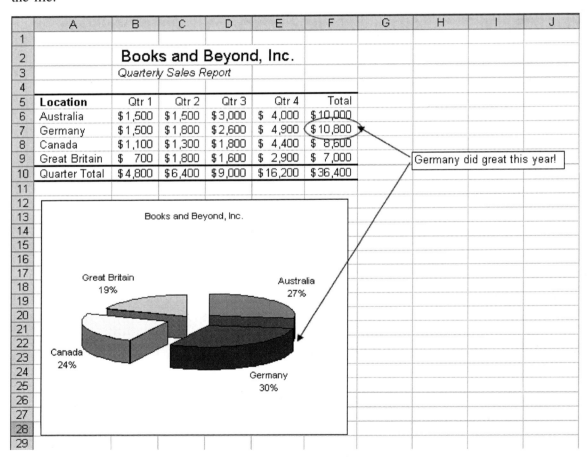

Figure 5-3: *My Objects.xls after the completion of the activity.*

What You Do	How You Do It
1. Resize the text box so that it fits the text and move it closer to the chart data.	a. Select the text box. b. Using the bottom-right sizing handle, **drag the box up and to the left. Size the box so that it fits the text.** Use Figure 5-3 as a guide. c. Move the text box so it is in cell H9.
2. Resize the arrow so that it goes from the text box in its new location to the Germany total in the chart data.	a. Select the arrow. b. Drag the right end of the arrow down to the text box.
3. Copy and paste the arrow and **resize and move it** so that it appears as it does in Figure 5-3. **Save the file** when you are finished.	a. Select the arrow. b. Press and hold [Ctrl] and drag the arrow down. c. With the arrow selected, **drag the right handle up to the text box. Drag the left handle down to the Germany pie slice.** Use Figure 5-3 as a guide. d. Save the file.

TOPIC C

Change the Order of Graphic Objects

Now that you know about creating and working with graphic objects, you will need to know how to change the order in which the graphic objects appear. In this topic, you will change the order of your graphic objects.

Imagine that you have created three graphic objects on your worksheet. You want one of those graphic object to be background only, but right now it is on top of the other objects and you can't see them. Well, you can change the order of your graphic objects and choose which objects appear on top and which appear on bottom.

Change the Order of Graphic Objects.

Procedure Reference: Change the Order of Graphic Objects

Sometimes when you are working with graphic objects, you want one object to appear on top of another. You do this by changing the order of the graphic objects. To change the order in which your graphic objects appear on your worksheet:

1. Select the object you want to change the order of.

2. Click the Draw button.

3. Choose Order and the appropriate order selection.

Order Options

There are four different options you can choose from when selecting an order for your graphic objects.

- *Bring to Front*: This option will bring the selected object in front of all graphic objects on the worksheet.

- *Send to Back*: This option will send the selected object to the back of all graphic objects on the worksheet.

- *Bring Forward*: This option brings the selected object forward once, in front of the nearest object.

- *Send Backward*: This option will send the selected object back one spot, behind the nearest object.

ACTIVITY 5-3

Changing the Order of your Graphic Objects

Setup:
The file My Objects.xls is open.

Scenario:
You want to create something behind the text box in your My Objects file that will draw attention to the text box. You have decided that you want to place a 16-point star behind the text box. When you are finished, save the file.

What You Do	How You Do It
1. Create a large, 16-point star over the text box.	a. On the Drawing toolbar, **click AutoShapes.**

b. **Choose Stars And Banners and select the
    16-point star.**

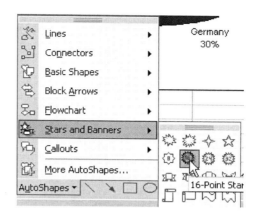

c. **Draw the star over the text box, making
    it large enough to cover the entire text
    box. Notice that the star obscures the
    text box.**

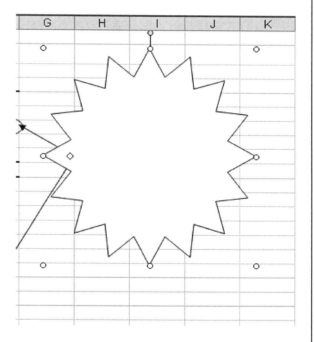

2. **Send the star to the back and bring
    the text box forward.**

a. **Select the star.**

b. **Click on Draw.**

c. **Choose Order→Send To Back.**

3. What has happened to the text box?

---

4. Move the star so that the text box is in the center. Save the file.

   a. Using the move handles, adjust the position of the star so that the text box appears in the middle of the star.

   b. Save the file.

TOPIC D

Group Graphic Objects

You know how to create and manipulate graphic objects. Now, you need to know how you can group multiple objects so that they essentially become one object. In this topic, you will group graphic objects.

Imagine that you have created multiple graphic objects. Now imagine that you want to move each of these graphic objects. They are positioned perfectly with each other, but they are all in the wrong place on the worksheet. So, you assume that you have to move them, one-by-one to their new position. Well, you're wrong. You can group these objects and move them all at once as one object.

Group Graphic Objects

Procedure Reference: Group Graphic Objects

To group graphic objects:

1. Select the first object you want to group.

2. Press and hold the [Ctrl] key and select the other objects you want to group together.

3. Click the Draw button.

4. Choose Group.

> To ungroup objects, right-click on any of the objects within the group and choose Grouping→ Ungroup.

ACTIVITY 5-4

Grouping your Graphic Objects

Setup:

My Objects.xls is open.

Scenario:

You have created many graphic objects in your worksheet (My Objects). You want to group the text box and the star that is behind it so that when you move them, they will move together. You also want to group the arrow with the text box and the star. You will then move the grouped object so that it is positioned exactly as you like and you will ungroup all of the objects. You will save the file when you are finished.

What You Do	How You Do It
1. Group the star, text box, and arrows together.	a. Select the star.
	b. Press and hold the [Ctrl] key.
	c. While still pressing [Ctrl], select the text box, and both arrows so that all four graphic objects are selected.
	d. Click Draw and wait for the menu to extend.
	e. Choose Group.
2. What happened when you grouped the objects?	
3. Move the grouped object so that it is positioned exactly as you like it.	a. Verify that the grouped object is selected.
	b. Drag the grouped object to a new position.
	c. Position the grouped object so that it is positioned correctly.
	d. Select each of the individual objects in the grouped object.

4. What happens when you try to select individual objects within a grouped object?

_____

5. Ungroup the objects and save the file.

   a. Select the grouped objects.

   b. Right-click on the grouped object and choose Grouping→Ungroup.

   c. Deselect the objects and save the file.

TOPIC E

Format Graphic Objects

Now that you know how to create graphic objects, you may find yourself wanting to change some of the properties of them. In this topic, you will format some of the graphic objects.

Once you have created graphic objects, you are not limited to the default settings. For example, you can remove or change the border around a text box. You can also change the color of any graphic object as well as rotate them.

Format Graphic Objects

Procedure Reference: Format Graphic Objects

To format any graphic object:

1. Display the Format AutoShape dialog box.

2. Using the various tabs, format the object as desired.

3. Click OK.

ACTIVITY 5-5

Formatting Graphic Objects

Setup:

My Objects.xls is open.

Scenario:

You want to add some formatting to your graphic objects in the file My Objects. First you want to eliminate the border on the text box and increase the font size of the text. You will then format the box so that it will automatically fit the text within it. You will then add a fill color of yellow to the text and finally add a fill color of the same yellow to the star. You will also increase the thickness of the star outline. Use Figure 5-4 as a guide. When you are finished, you will save the file.

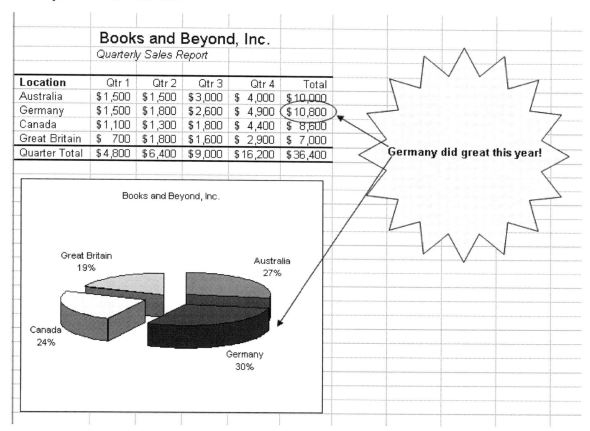

Figure 5-4: *My Objects.xls after the activity has been completed.*

Lesson 5

What You Do	How You Do It
1. Format the text box so that there is no border, the font is bold, and the fill is yellow. Also format the text box so that it is sized automatically and the text is vertically and horizontally centered.	a. Select the text box.
	b. Right-click and choose Format Text Box.
	c. On the Font tab, in the Font Style list box, select Bold.
⚠ When you select the text box, you must make sure that the box is selected, and it is not in edit mode. If the text box is in edit mode, you will not be able to format anything other than the text.	d. Select the Alignment tab.
	e. In the Text Alignment section, set both the Horizontal and Vertical alignments to Center.
	f. Check the Automatic Size check box.
	g. On the Colors And Lines tab, from the Fill Color drop-down list, select yellow. From the Line Color drop-down list, select No Line.
	h. Click OK.
	i. Adjust the position of the text box so it is in the center of the star.
2. Format the star so that its fill color is the same as the text box and it has a 1 pt outline. Save the file.	a. Select the star.
	b. Right-click on the star and choose Format AutoShape.
	c. On the Colors And Lines tab, from the Fill Color drop-down list, select the same yellow that is filling the text box.
	d. Change the Line Weight to 1pt.
	e. Click OK.
	f. Save the file.

TOPIC F

Insert Clip Art

Another way to enhance your worksheet is to add clip art. In this topic you will locate and insert clip art into your worksheet.

More than likely, at some point when working with Excel, you will want to insert some clip art. Using clip art can enhance your worksheets by adding visual appeal to them.

What are Clips?

Clips are files that are provided with Excel for you to use in your worksheets. These can include art (pictures), sounds, animation, or mini-movies. All of these items are contained in the clip organizer which is an Office program that contains all of these files. They can all be accessed using the Insert Clip Art task pane. In this topic you will be working with the art that is contained in the clip organizer. This is called Clip Art.

Insert Clip Art

Procedure Reference: Insert Clip Art

To insert clip art into your worksheet:

1. Display the task pane.

2. Click the Other Task Panes drop-down arrow and choose Insert Clip Art.

3. In the Search For text box, type a description of the clip art you are looking for.

4. Click Search.

5. Drag the picture from the results box to your worksheet.

Search for Clip Art

When you want to use a piece of clip art, you must first search for it in the Insert Clip Art task pane. To do this, type a keyword that describes the clip art you want in the Search Text text box of the Insert Clip Art task pane. Click on the Search button and you will see what the results are.

ACTIVITY 5-6

Inserting Clip Art

Setup:
My Objects.xls is open.

Scenario:
Before you present your worksheet to your co-workers, you would like to add some clip art, just to make it more visually appealing. You will search for a book clip art and insert any one of the images into the worksheet. You will then move the clip art next to the worksheet title, using Figure 5-5 as a guide. When you are finished, you will save the file.

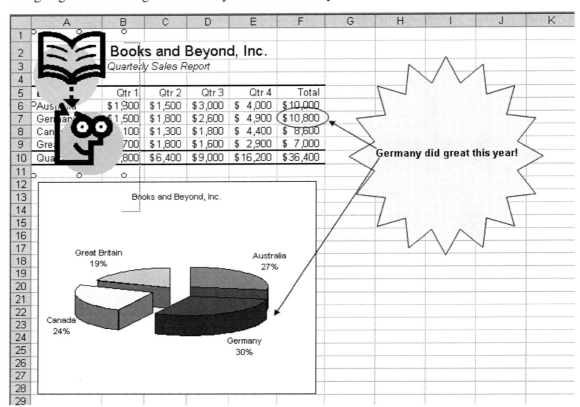

Figure 5-5: *My Objects.xls after the activity is complete.*

What You Do	How You Do It

1. Search for clip art using the keyword books.

   a. Choose View→Toolbars→Task Pane.

   b. On the task pane, **click on the Other Task Panes down arrow and choose Insert Clip Art.**

   c. If necessary, in the Organizer message box, **click Do It Now.**

   d. In the Search For text box, **type** *books* **and press [Enter].**

 You will resize the clip art in the next activity.

2. **Insert the second clip art and place it next to the worksheet title. Save the file.**

   a. **Move your mouse pointer over the second clip art.**

   b. **Drag the clip art from the task pane to the top of the worksheet so the top left corner is located in cell A1.**

   c. **Save the file.**

LESSON 5

TOPIC G

Modify Clip Art

Now that you know how to insert clip art, you will want to know how to modify it and make changes to that clip art. In this topic, you will modify clip art by sizing it and changing the color scheme.

Many people think that once you have inserted your clip art there is little you can do to change the look of that clip art. Well, you can resize it and you can also change the colors in the clip art. You aren't stuck with whatever the clip art gives you. You now have the ability to modify and customize the clip art.

What Can You Modify in Clip Art?

When you insert a clip art from the clip gallery, you can change some of the attributes of the clip art. You can use the Picture toolbar, which is displayed in Figure 5-6, to adjust the appearance of the picture. Following is a table that describes the tools on the Picture toolbar, and how they change the picture.

Figure 5-6: *The Picture toolbar.*

Tool	Description
	The Insert Picture From File button allows you to insert a picture of your own from an existing file.
	The Color button allows you to change the color from Automatic to grayscale, black and white, or washout (which has the effect of a watermark).
	The More Contrast and Less Contrast buttons allow you to adjust the contrast of the clip art.
	The More Brightness and Less Brightness buttons allow you to adjust the brightness of the clip art.
	The Crop button allows you to select and remove part of the clip art.
	The Rotate Left button allows you to rotate the image 90 degrees at a time.
	The Line Style button allows you to add a border to the clip art and adjust the line style of the border.
	The Compress Pictures button allows you to make the clip art file size smaller, thereby taking up less memory and space on your computer when you save the file.

Tool	Description
	The Format Picture button opens the Format Picture dialog box, which allows you to change the color and lines of the border, the size of the clip art, the color contrast and brightness of the clip art and to protect the clip art.
	The Set Transparent Color button allows you to create a transparent area in the picture and set the color of that transparent area.
	The Reset Picture button allows you to reset the clip art back to the way it was when you first inserted it.

Modify your Clip Art

Procedure Reference: Modify Your Clip Art

To modify your clip art:

1. Select the clip art you want to modify.

2. Open the Format Picture dialog box.

3. Make the changes to your clip art as desired.

4. Click OK.

ACTIVITY 5-7

Modifying your Clip Art

Setup:
The file My Objects.xls is open.

Scenario:
You have inserted your clip art into your My Objects worksheet. First you size the clip art so that it fits next to the worksheet title. Then you want to add a fill color and a border to the image, using Figure 5-7 as a guide. When you are finished, you will save and close the file.

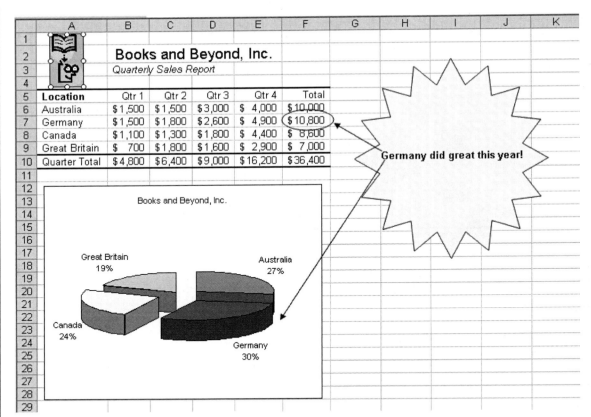

Figure 5-7: *My Objects.xls after the activity has been completed.*

What You Do	How You Do It
1. **Resize the clip art so that it fits next to the worksheet title.**	a. **Select the clip art.**
	b. **Place your mouse pointer on the bottom-right sizing handle and drag up and to the left until the image fits in the range A1:A4.**
2. **Format the clip art so that there is a light gray fill and there is a 0.5 border around the image.**	a. **Right-click on the clip art image.**
	b. **Choose Format Picture.**
	c. **Select the Colors And Lines tab.**
	d. **From the Fill Color drop-down list, select a light shade of gray.**
	e. **From the Line Color drop-down list, select Automatic and adjust the weight to 0.5.**
	f. **Click OK.**

3. Save and close the file.

    a. Save the file.

    b. Close the file.

Lesson 5 Follow-up

In this lesson you learned how to enhance your worksheet using graphic objects. First you created the graphic objects, then you resized, moved, and copied them. You also grouped and formatted your graphic objects. Finally, you inserted and formatted clip art.

1. How will you use graphic objects in your worksheets?

2. Which graphic objects do you think you will use the most?

Follow-up

In this course you learned how to customize your workbook, work with multiple data sources, and collaborate with others using shared workbooks. You also learned how to enhance your worksheets using charts and graphic objects. You are now able to customize your workspace and your workbooks and use multiple data sources efficiently.

What's Next?

Excel 2002: Level 3 is the last course in the Excel 2002 series.

APPENDIX A

Microsoft Office Specialist Program

Selected Element K courseware addresses Microsoft Office Specialist skills. The following tables indicate where Excel 2002 skills are covered. For example, 1-3 indicates the lesson and activity number applicable to that skill.

Core Skill Sets and Skills Being Measured	Excel 2002: Level 1	Excel 2002: Level 2	Excel 2002: Level 3
Working with Cells and Cell Data			
Insert, delete, and move cells	2-1, 2-6, 4-10		
Enter and edit cell data including text, numbers, and formulas	1-2, 1-4, 2-6, 3-1, 3-3, 3-5, 3-6, 4-1, 4-2, 4-3, 4-4, 4-5, 4-6, 4-7, 4-8, 4-9, 4-10, 4-11		
Check spelling		1-4	
Find and replace cell data and formats	2-7, 4-7, 4-10		
Work with a subset of data by filtering lists		2-4	
Managing Workbooks			
Manage workbook files and folders	1-6, 2-1		
Create workbooks using templates		1-1	
Save workbooks using different names and file formats	1-2, 1-6, 3-1		
Formatting and Printing Worksheets			
Apply and modify cell formats	1-5, 4-1, 4-2, 4-3, 4-4, 4-5, 4-6, 4-7, 4-8, 4-9, 4-10, 4-11		
Modify row and column settings	2-4, 7-1	3-3	

Core Skill Sets and Skills Being Measured	Excel 2002: Level 1	Excel 2002: Level 2	Excel 2002: Level 3
Modify row and column formats	4-8, 4-9		
Apply styles	4-4		
Use automated tools to format worksheets	4-11		
Modify Page Setup options for worksheets	7-2, 7-3, 7-4, 7-5, 7-7		
Preview and print worksheets and workbooks	7-7	3-1	
Modifying Workbooks			
Insert and delete worksheets	5-4		
Modify worksheet names and positions	5-1, 5-2		
Use 3-D references		4-1	
Creating and Revising Formulas			
Create and revise formulas	3-1, 3-2, 3-3, 3-5, 3-6		
Use statistical, data and time, financial, and logical functions in formulas	3-1, 3-3	4-3, 4-5	
Creating and Modifying Graphics			
Create, modify, position and print charts	6-1, 6-3		
Create, modify and position graphics		1-3	
Workgroup Collaboration			
Convert worksheets into web pages		3-4	
Create hyperlinks		6-1	
View and edit comments		6-2, 6-3, 6-4	

Expert Skill Sets And Skills Being Measured	Excel 2002: Level 1	Excel 2002: Level 2	Excel 2002: Level 3
Importing and Exporting Data			
Import data to Excel		3-1, 3-2	
Export data from Excel		3-3	
Publish worksheets and work-books to the Web		3-5	
Managing Workbooks			
Create, edit, and apply templates		1-2, 1-3, 1-4	
Create workspaces			2-1
Use Data Consolidation			2-2, 2-4
Formatting Numbers			

Expert Skill Sets And Skills Being Measured	Excel 2002: Level 1	Excel 2002: Level 2	Excel 2002: Level 3
Create and apply custom number formats	4-2		
Use conditional formats			1-1
Working with Ranges			
Use named ranges in formulas		4-2	
Use Lookup and Reference functions		4-4	
Customizing Excel			
Customize toolbars and menus			1-3, 1-4
Create, edit, and run macros			1-5, 1-7
Auditing Worksheets			
Audit formulas		4-6, 4-7	
Locate and resolve errors		4-8	
Identify dependencies in formulas		4-6, 4-7, 4-8	
Summarizing Data			
Use subtotals with lists and ranges		2-3	
Define and apply filters		2-5	
Add group and outline criteria to ranges			1-7
Use data validation			1-2
Retrieve external data and create queries			2-7
Create Extensible Markup Language (XML) Web queries			2-9
Analyzing Data			
Create PivotTables, PivotCharts, and PivotTable/PivotChart Reports		5-1, 5-2	
Forecast values with *what-if* analysis		4-4	
Create and display scenarios		5-3	
Workgroup Collaboration			
Modify passwords, protections, and properties			3-1, 3-2
Create a shared workbook			3-3
Track, accept, and reject changes to workbooks			3-4, 3-7
Merge workbooks			3-6

NOTES

LESSON LABS

Due to classroom setup constraints, some labs cannot be keyed in sequence immediately following their associated lesson. Your instructor will tell you whether your labs can be practiced immediately following the lesson or whether they require separate setup from the main lesson content.

LESSON 1 LAB 1

Customizing Your Workbook

Data Files:

- Practice Customizing.xls

Scenario:

You have a file (Practice Customizing) that you want to add some customization to. First, you will add conditional formatting so that any travel expense total above $2000 is italicized and red. Then, you will create your own menu and add some of the menu items you use frequently. You will also add and remove buttons from the toolbars. Finally, you will create a macro that adds formatting to the worksheet.

---

1. Add conditional formatting to the April travel totals so that any total that is above $2000 will appear italicized and the font is red.

---

2. Create a custom menu, and add the Close, Open, and Save commands to the new menu.

---

3. Remove Open and Save buttons from the toolbars. Add a button of your choice. When you are finished, **make sure you reset the toolbars and menus for the next lesson.**

---

4. Create a macro that adds some formatting to the worksheet title. When you have finished creating the macro, **run it on the May worksheet.**

Lesson Labs

5. When you are finished, **save the file as** *My Practice Customizing* **and close the file.**

LESSON 2 LAB 1

Workspaces, Exporting, and Web Queries

Data Files:

- Practice Flanders.xls
- Practice Smith.xls
- Practice Tanor.xls

Scenario:

Before you begin working in your worksheets, you want to create a workspace from three workbooks (Practice Smith.xls, Practice Tanor.xls, Practice Flanders.xls) that you use frequently at the same time. Once you have created a workspace, you want to export the Practice Flanders workbook into an XML document. When you have done that, you will create a Web query in the Practice Smith file and query a Web site of your choice.

1. **Create a workspace using the three files.**

2. **Export the Practice Flanders workbooks as XML data, saving the XML file as** *My Practice XML.*

3. **Create a Web query in the Practice Smith file, and query data from a Web site of your choice.**

LESSON 3 LAB 1

Protecting and Sharing Your Workbooks

Data Files:

- Practice Collaborating.xls

Scenario:

You have a worksheet called Practice Collaborating.xls that you would like to have some co-workers take a look at. Before you share your worksheet, you want to protect all the formulas in your workbook. Then you will save the file as a shared workbook.

1. In the file Practice Collaborating, **protect the worksheet so that all of the formulas can not be edited. Add an error message of your choice.**

2. **Save the file as a shared workbook called *My Practice Collaborating*.**

3. **Close the file.**

LESSON 4 LAB 1

Practice Advanced Charting

Scenario:

You have some data that you want to chart in the Practice Chart file. First, you are going to create a column chart based on the Australia and Germany data on a new chart sheet. Then you are going to change the baseball caps data series by adding some custom formatting. Finally, you will move the legend to the top of the chart.

1. **Create a column chart based on the Australia and Germany data on a new chart sheet.**

2. **Change the baseball caps data series by adding some formatting.**

3. **Move the legend to the top of the page.**

4. **Save the file as *My Practice Chart* and close the file.**

LESSON 5 LAB 1

Practice Using Objects

Data Files:

- Practice Objects.xls

Scenario:

You have a worksheet that you need to use for a presentation called Practice Objects.xls. You want to point out that the reason the German division didn't do so well is because it was added late in the year. So, you are going to draw an AutoShape arrow to the Germany pie slice and add a text box near that arrow that explains that the Germany division was added after the third quarter. Then you will add a clip art relating to amusement parks to the top of your worksheet. When you are finished, save the file as My Practice Objects and close the file.

1. **Create an arrow using autoshapes that goes from the Germany pie slice to an empty part of the worksheet.**

2. **Add a text box next to the arrow that says *Germany wasn't added until the middle of the third quarter*.**

3. **Search for and add a clip art that is related to amusement parks.**

4. **Save the file as *My Practice Objects* and close the file.**

SOLUTIONS

Lesson 1

Activity 1-2

3. What happens when you select a cell and try to enter some text, rather than a number into one of the data cells?

    A comment type message telling you what you should enter in the cell is displayed when you first select the cell. When you try and enter text rather than a number into one of the cells, the error message that you created is displayed.

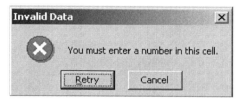

Activity 1-7

1. In the file, Product Sales.xls, what are some of the different ways you might like to view this information?

    Answers will vary.

3. Using Table 1-1 as a guide, identify each of the outline symbols. Which symbols do you think you will use the most when you use the outlining feature?

    Answers will vary.

Lesson 2

Activity 2-3

1. What does cell C8 contain? How does the range appear that is included in the formula?

    Cell C8 contains the formula =SUM(C5:C7). The range C5:C7 is hidden in the outline.

3. What do cells C5, C6, and C7 contain?

    Cell C5 contains a link to the Hanover workbook. Cell C6 contains a link to the Jaen workbook, and cell C7 contains a link to the Monder workbook.

SOLUTIONS

Activity 2-4

2. **What information on the three sheets in Category Consolidation.xls is similar, and what is different?**

   The type of data that the worksheets contain is similar, however, the location in which the similar information is displayed is different on each sheet. Some worksheets contain information that is unique to itself, while some worksheets contain data that is similar to the other worksheets.

4. **What effect did the consolidation have on the worksheet.**

   The data from the other worksheets was placed on this worksheet.

Activity 2-5

2. **What are the similarities between the Finch, Decker, Simpson, and Summary workbooks?**

   Each workbook is setup identically. Each worksheet shows an item code, item price, and quantity sold for 10 items. Each worksheet also calculates the total sales and the commission for each item.

5. **What has happened to the contents of cell A5 on the Summary worksheet?**

   A formula that sums the content of cell D15 in each worksheet has been entered into cell A5. A5 now contains the Total sales figure.

Activity 2-6

3. **What has happened to cell A5 in the New Summary workbook?**

   The references to Simpson has now been changed to Sandeford.

Activity 2-7

4. **What does the file look like?**

   The XML text is similar to HTML text and there are tags that indicated some of the structure and appearance of the worksheet.

Activity 2-8

2. **What do you notice about the imported file?**

   There is no formatting in the imported file, but the text and location of the text is intact.

Lesson 3

Activity 3-1

5. **What happens when you try to make a change to the formula? What happens when you try to resize the graphic object?**

    You are able to select the locked cells containing formulas, but when you try to edit the contents of the cell a message appears saying that the cell is protected and is read-only. When you try to resize the graphic, you aren't even able to select it.

Activity 3-2

3. **What happens when you try to change the position of the worksheets?**

    The mouse pointer changes to a circle with a line through it and you cannot change the position of the worksheets.

Activity 3-7

3. **What information is displayed in the Accept Or Reject Changes window when it locates a change?**

    It displays the name of the person who changed it, the date and time that it was changed, and what the cell contained before it was changed.

Lesson 5

Activity 5-3

3. **What has happened to the text box?**

    The text box now appear on top of the star and the star is underneath the text box. The arrow lines also appear and the star is under them as well.

Activity 5-4

2. **What happened when you grouped the objects?**

    The individual fill handles disappeared and were replaced by a single set of fill handles that surround all the graphic objects.

4. **What happens when you try to select individual objects within a grouped object?**

    You are able to select the individual objects, just as you could before the objects were grouped.

NOTES

GLOSSARY

conditional formatting
Formatting that Excel applies automatically to a specified cell if the criteria of the conditions set are met.

dependant workbook
A workbook containing a formula that links it to another workbook.

external reference
A reference to another workbook or to a defined name in another workbook.

macro
A macro is a group of user-created instructions that automates one or more operations.

source workbook
A workbook to which a formula refers.

Sub procedure
A named combination of VBA code that is executed as a unit.

Visual Basic Editor
The window you use to view, create, and modify VBA code.

Visual Basic for Applications
The computer programming language that you use to create macros in Excel.

workspace
A workspace is an Excel file that includes several workbooks.

NOTES

INDEX

Looking for media files?

They are now conveniently located at www.elementk.com/courseware-file-downloads

Downloading is quick and easy:

1. Visit www.elementk.com/courseware-file-downloads
2. In the search field, type in either the part number or the title
3. Of the courseware titles displayed, choose your title by clicking on the name
4. Links to the data files are located in the middle of the screen
5. Follow the instructions on the screen based upon your web browser

Note that there may be other files available for download in addition to the course files.

Approximate download times:

The amount of time it takes to download your data files will vary according to the file's size and your Internet connection speed. A broadband connection is highly recommended. The average time to download a 10 mb file on a broadband connection is less than 1 minute.